Walk by ~
Jason Karr

Merry Xmas
Dave
Love You
Cindy
"2015"

Lessons in Living and Dying

Reflections on a Life Well Lived

DIANN PASS

WESTBOW
PRESS®
A DIVISION OF THOMAS NELSON
& ZONDERVAN

All scripture taken from New King James Version unless noted. Copyright © 1979, 1980, 1982 by Thomas Nelson, Inc. Used by permission. All rights reserved.

Scripture quotations taken from the New American Standard Bible®, Copyright © 1960, 1962, 1963, 1968, 1971, 1972, 1973, 1975, 1977, 1995 by The Lockman Foundation. Used by permission. (www.Lockman.org)

Scripture quotations are from The Holy Bible, English Standard Version® (ESV®), copyright © 2001 by Crossway, a publishing ministry of Good News Publishers. Used by permission. All rights reserved.

WestBow Press books may be ordered through booksellers or by contacting:

WestBow Press
A Division of Thomas Nelson & Zondervan
1663 Liberty Drive
Bloomington, IN 47403
www.westbowpress.com
1 (866) 928-1240

Because of the dynamic nature of the Internet, any web addresses or links contained in this book may have changed since publication and may no longer be valid. The views expressed in this work are solely those of the author and do not necessarily reflect the views of the publisher, and the publisher hereby disclaims any responsibility for them.

Cover photo taken by the author.

ISBN: 978-1-5127-1067-0 (sc)
ISBN: 978-1-5127-1068-7 (hc)
ISBN: 978-1-5127-1066-3 (e)

Library of Congress Control Number: 2015914360

Print information available on the last page.

WestBow Press rev. date: 9/24/2015

These stories are written in memory of a special man whose life has been an inspiration to many. In the Old Testament, God urged His people to stack stones into a monument as a remembrance. These stories are a monument, and I have named the monument Faithful to memorialize God's faithfulness in a life.

Contents

Foreword

To me John Pass, like John Wayne, was bigger than life. John Pass was a man's man, a man of honor, a cowboy, smooth and handsome, a true gentleman, a champion for those who had less than him, and most important of all, a godly man. As a young college graduate I got to know him in the early '70s because of my friendship with his son J.T., the apple that didn't fall far from the tree. John's charisma and genuine love for people spilled over and infected everyone that he employed or befriended. I'm proud to have been one of those infected. He was the first *cool* dad I ever met. After every encounter with John, I tried to take away something from him that would make me a better person like him. But this book's story is not just about John. It's a story about a wife who loved unconditionally. It's a story about an imperfect family that found the perfect love of Christ. Now they all rejoice that after years of suffering, John has been healed, and that because he believed, he has taken his rightful place at the feet of his heavenly Father. Again I say *rejoice*.

Ron Hall
Author of New York Times best seller *Same Kind of Different as Me*

Acknowledgments

I express my gratitude to the members of Midland Bible Church who loved us, cared for us, served us, prayed for us tirelessly in the years of John's illness, and now continue to love on me. They remain the family I have chosen for myself. Most of the stories in this book come from experiences with the wonderful brothers and sisters in Christ from Midland Bible. However, I also thank my family, who have shown me great love, helping my heart to heal, and my grandchildren, who bring joy to my life and a smile to my days.

I also thank Brandon Shuman for his excellent contribution in assisting me to clearly express myself and Barbara Braithwaite for encouragement to write. I am grateful as well to the "readers" who caught my mistakes! Gretchen Keene at Westbow Press, thank you for encouraging me to complete the project!

Many thanks to Tim and Terri Dunn. Tim, for your teaching of God's Word that gives me confidence as a chaplain. And Terri, for your friendship.

Thank you, Vince and Gail Loftis, for always being there. Vince, you walked with me through the valley of the shadow of death and beyond. And Gail you generously shared Vince with us and many others through the years.

Lisa Frosch, thank you for all you did to make the pictures beautiful and always for your friendship. You and Tim were always there. Betty Rae and Paul, thank you for your love and friendship.

Jenny and Chris, thanks for all the lunches, pies, and laughs! Huevos?

Tina and Joe – you walked the final mile with us.

Most of all, thanks to Christ for adoption into His family and giving my life meaning.

Introduction:
A Man Worth Knowing

The world lost an incredible man on 12-12-12. John Pass was a man loved by all who knew him, lo, all who came into contact with him—as evidenced by the full church at his memorial service. You see, John was eighty-six when he died. Usually, services for people in their eighties are held in cemeteries because by that age, most of the people's friends and family are either deceased or have one foot in the grave and the other on a banana peel.

Not so with John. John had friends in their twenties, thirties, forties, fifties, and from there it began to narrow. Some people at his service flew into Midland, Texas, in their private jets. A couple of young men in their mid-forties, who had known John since age nine, drove in from hundreds of miles away. One of them drove six hours, stayed two hours, and drove the six hours back to return to work. John's barber came. The pharmacist also. And Elaine, counter girl from the cleaners. There were men in their sixties whom John had given their first job out of college. Also present were the boys who had lived across the alley, now in their sixties. One of them spoke at the service, telling stories of days past with John, whom they had kept up with their entire lives. Two years later, I still have men approach me and tell stories of John, and more importantly, lessons they learned from him. So the question is what makes a life extraordinary? I hope these reflections will provide insight, inspiration, and lessons for life so that you, too, can lead an extraordinary life.

. . . . and even though he is dead, he still speaks.

—Hebrews 11:4 NASB

God Is Good

Whenever anyone exchanged greetings with John, his standard answer when asked was "If it was any better I couldn't stand it." He was nothing if not positive. Everyone loved to be around him because he never had a negative thing to say.

More than that, everyone wanted to be around him because he made you feel important. He looked directly into your eyes and never looked away—regardless of who might walk into a room or walk right behind you. He interviewed you—asking questions about you, never talking about himself. And he remembered. John would be able to recall details of your life and then ask about your children, your golf game, how the hunting trip went, with sincere interest.

John never met a stranger. Once we were in San Francisco at a really stuffy party. I was not particularly enjoying the experience. The people all seemed pretentious: looking down their noses, asking "What do you *do?*" John was engaged in a conversation with an older gentleman, maybe eighty years old, who was the Austrian consul. They were discussing languages and how many the man spoke. John divulged that his grandparents were all German, and he recalled a nursery song his mother sang to him in German. The next thing I knew, they were both belting out that nursery song together in full voice! They drew a lot of attention. People were smiling broadly. Suddenly, that formal party was not so stiff any longer. Laughter pealed through the room.

On December 12, 2011, John and I traveled to Dallas to see the pulmonologist who was treating John's emphysema. The trip to Dallas was five and a half hours and was getting more difficult each time we made it. John was still doing the driving, at the age of eighty-five, and was still a pretty decent driver; but life was getting discernibly more difficult overall for him. We had a late-afternoon appointment and didn't see the doctor until about five o'clock. Prior to that John had already been to the lab and had performed breathing tests so the doctor would have the results when we arrived. John's doctor (I'll call him Dr. Jones here) was a large man, imposing. He was bald on top with wiry gray hair around the sides and back of his head. He was an extremely busy man—head of pulmonology at the med school, a teacher, and a practicing physician. He had tried hard not to like John, or more specifically, he had tried to keep a polite distance. But John was having none of it. During prior visits, Dr. Jones had eventually disclosed that he went to a Presbyterian church; that he had three children, all at the same Texas university; and that he loved to play golf in Austin, Texas.

On that day, Dr. Jones came into the exam room and walked around John's wheelchair. (John hated the wheelchair, but I had insisted he use it because the building was so large. I knew he did not have the strength to navigate that huge building on foot.) John began to rise from the chair to get up onto the examining table. Dr. Jones put his hand on John's shoulder and said to just sit there. The doctor walked around the wheelchair, listening to John's heart and lungs, resting a hand gently on John's shoulders as he did the exam.

Upon completing his examination, the doctor said, "Mr. Pass, there is nothing more we can do for you." The doctor turned to me and said that I could call him on his cell phone, text him, or e-mail him, but he felt that the trip was too much to ask John to make again. Wow. There was absolute silence in the room. The moment was surreal. My mind raced to grasp the implications—no, the reality—of what had just been said. Then, as he always did, Dr. Jones shook John's hand, then mine, and turned to leave the room.

John spoke. "Doctor, can I ask you a question?"

"Well, certainly, Mr. Pass."

My eyes stung with unshed tears. My mouth was dry. Tension in the room was palpable. John had never before asked his prognosis. I think both the doctor and I were expecting a question like How long do I have? But no—instead John asked, "When do the kids come home for Christmas?" And "How are the Presbyterians?" Then, finally, "How is your golf game?"

I was stunned. Surely John did not understand what the doctor was saying to him.

The doctor answered each question, and as he turned to leave, I saw a tear in the corner of his eye. Then it hit me. John was just being John. He fully understood. In his darkest hour, John still put others before himself. This was John's way of saying good-bye. The die was cast, and I got a glimpse into the future—a future that was rushing at me, unwanted and unwelcome.

When John and I reached the car outside, it was cold, dark, and raining. I sat down in the driver's seat, but I was still processing the information we had just received. I gripped the steering wheel, staring straight ahead.

In the darkness I heard John say, "God has been so good to me. I have had such a good life."

Yes, God had been good to both of us. John died one year later, to the day.

God is good, all the time.
All the time, God is good.

For the LORD is good;
His mercy is everlasting,
And His truth endures to all generations.

—Psalm 100:5

By All Appearances

John was a handsome man. A friend of more than thirty years always referred to John as a movie star. He had a Clark Gable quality. As far back as I can remember, John had graying hair. I'm guessing he had much less gray when I first knew him, but honestly, I always saw him the same. He never aged in my eyes. And I think he aged very well and never lost that movie star quality.

If John had been a woman, I would have described him as looking "right out of the band box." I'm not certain exactly what that old cliché means, but for me, it describes the attention John gave to every detail of his appearance. There were few days in our years together when John was not showered, shaved, and looking quite dapper. His attention to his appearance was not out of some kind of vanity. It was just who he was, part of his commitment to be the best he could be every day of his life.

John's eyes were hazel and had a sparkle that was unmistakable—not the sparkle of a mischievous boy, but more the sparkle of delight in life. His hair, which had once been black, was brindled with gray. John was a man's man. He never worked out with weights or muscled up, but he definitely leaned more toward sports than books. While

John did not look like an athlete, he was a quite good golfer. He was physically coordinated. One day he picked up a tennis racquet while dressed in his suit and leather shoes and returned a hard serve from our sixteen-year-old son—who was more than a little surprised.

John liked hunting and horses and cows and outdoor activities. When we had a ranch, he would be found dressed in jeans, almost white from the washing, with the hems gnawed away in the back from his walking in the ever-present boots. He might be wearing a "gimme" cap (a visored cap with some organization's logo) or a felt or straw western hat, according to season. John had belt buckles made for each of the two of us. They were silver with a scrolled design—his with the initials JP and mine with DP. Those were the buckles we wore with our jeans. John had quite an array of boots—black and gray and butterscotch and chocolate. Some had hides of alligator, crocodile, ostrich, snake, or lizard. Also, there were "ranch boots," those old favorites that had stepped in the mud and the cow patties and gone through the briars and cactuses.

The thing John wore that I loved the most was his smile. His smile did not just beam; it radiated and warmed you when it settled on you. When John shook someone's hand, he never *just* shook the hand. He placed his other hand on the person's shoulder or elbow. It was almost like getting a hug when he shook your hand. As he shook your hand, he was repeating your name and asking you a question designed to help him remember you. "How long have you lived here?" "Where do you play golf?" "Tell me about your family." Then, John would repeat your name at least one more time. After that, he knew he would remember you. Next time John saw you, he would go back to those original questions and ask how your golf game was going or what your kids (by name) were doing. John never forgot any detail, and he realized how important we feel when we are called by name or the details of our life are remembered.

Yes, John was handsome, but he never stood and primped before the mirror. He liked a pretty shirt and tie, but John knew that the clothes do not make the man. The man makes the clothes.

For the LORD does not see as man sees; for man looks at the outward appearance, but The LORD looks at the heart.

—1 Samuel 16:7

Choose Life

John was always cheerful, sometimes ridiculously so, almost Pollyanna. Everyone who knew John loved that he was always cheerful, always upbeat, even in the face of adversity, always looking for the positive. Sometimes I heckled him, calling myself a realist. My daughter hated his boisterous good mornings when we were first married. It had been nine years since her father and I divorced. She had lived during that time with me, the realist. Now she was faced with Mr. Happy every morning, and she wasn't exactly a morning person—always late for school, disorganized, a little frayed as she gulped down her breakfast and lunged for the door.

Everyone at the office called John "Mr. Pass". Really. And they said it in a respectful, hushed tone. He loved it. He loved being the Big Guy. He had worked hard for everything he had. He had come a long way since those days when he wore overalls to school while the other boys wore trousers. John did not want to look and feel like a hick. So at age nine, John began throwing the newspaper, every morning and every evening, to pay for those trousers he wanted. He never whined or complained that he was mistreated; he just went to work and did what it took to accomplish his goal. That was a paradigm for his later achievements in life.

Meanwhile, I had entered the picture. I loved to give him a hard time. It was fun. I would call his office and ask for the head turkey. He was horrified and asked, laughing, that I not do that anymore. I responded that I always reached him, so apparently his office knew who the head turkey was. With me in his life, he dropped that reserved persona, but he gained something better: a type of fan club. He was still the Big Guy, but he had a new name. My kids dubbed him Big Sir—a title fitting for the man he was.

John and I had a seven-year courtship and then married. Those were glorious years in many ways. We were certainly living large, as my son would say, but what I loved the most, and I know John did too, was just our time together—John, myself, and my two children. Dinners together were fun. Sometimes in their conversations, John and my son would break into gales of laughter for no discernible reason. But my daughter and I would usually wind up laughing with them. Their joy was contagious, and we all thrived.

Family vacations were fun, too. We all cherished them. There was never a time when the kids were ashamed of us or didn't want to be with us. I saw it in other teenagers, but never in ours. John set the tone, and the kids and I loved our family time together as well. My daughter even began to enjoy those boisterous good morning greetings.

Then, there were the lean years. The years John did not expect. All had seemed so secure in his world; it was surprising to see all the results of his hard work derailed.

Through all those hard times, we were virtually glued together, closer than before. The hardship made us stronger. Often, one or the other of us would comment what a great team we were.

We *were* a great team because we had a great leader. John always had a strong direction. He never wavered in his vision to provide for our family. More than that, John provided the foundation of optimism that took us through the lean times.

That optimism became great faith as John reconnected with the faith of his childhood. It was a faith that grew and matured; it took us through those lean times and even more so through the later years of John's failing health. There was a long, narrow road of challenges after his diagnosis of emphysema. Emphysema is a terrible, hopeless disease. From the outset, the doctors give the person no hope. It is a minimally treatable illness, but an illness that robs one of all hope and of any personal pride. It robs all breath both literally and figuratively—and in the end, life itself.

That hopelessness could be pretty depressing if one focused on it. John never did. He laughed. He loved. He almost never talked about his health or even himself. He chose, moment by moment, to see all that is good.

You see, life is a choice. Each person has the privilege to decide how to live his or her life. We can choose. John taught our family, and many other men by example, to choose a life of love and service, a life of optimism in the face of great difficulty.

> Therefore, choose life that both you and your descendants may live.

> —Deuteronomy 30:19 ESV

The New Man

It's funny how plainly I see John now. I lived with him for more than twenty-eight years. While I knew him intimately, I have come to know him better after his death.

John was a proud man. He had worked hard all his life. When I first knew him, he was young, robust, and ever so proud. But life has a way of humbling a person, doesn't it? At age sixty, life stepped in and took away all our financial security. We still had all our personal stuff, but all the money in the bank was gone; ranch—gone; condo in Colorado—gone; huge estate where we lived—gone; pride—gone. Those were hard, hard years. Gone also was the vehicle for making money after John closed his twenty-five-year-old business.

A lesser man (in fact, probably most men) would have coasted until age sixty-five and then collected social security—maybe never working again. Not John. He worked. He dug deep within himself. His dream was to have it again—not all the stuff, but the financial security.

It took fifteen years to have that financial security again. But we would never again desire the excessive indulgence in worldly possessions we once had. We got something better.

I can remember living in that rented duplex we moved to when we sold our home. I loved that place. It was old and beautiful, if a little tired. It had all the luxury of the sixty-five years in the past when it was first built—beautiful marble bathrooms and expansive living and dining rooms. A foyer that was large enough for the baby grand piano. But a tiny, outdated, secluded kitchen.

What we got from the transition was a new appreciation for what we had—we had each other. We loved each other, but all the glitz was gone—the glamorous parties and fancy vacations. We were both working sixty- to seventy-hour weeks. We had a new peace. And John had something new for him: humility. Not a false pretense at being humble, but a real, soul-baring humility.

It didn't come immediately. He grew into it. At first he felt uncomfortable in his new skin. He sought after the old things—Scripture calls it the old man. He wanted to recoup it all. But gradually, he settled into and accepted our new life; he made lemonade.

The fancy cars were gone. The prestige of owning his own company was also gone, but a peace had washed over our home. The peace that passes understanding came to live in our hearts. We had to figure out how to pay two college tuitions. We had to deal with cars that wore out, and more simply, shoes that wore out. We had to learn to depend on God. This was very humbling for a man who had always been able to provide in big ways.

Then, we learned that there are even greater humbling forces, such as losing one's health. John detested the oxygen device for his emphysema. It embarrassed him. It was a picture that he was not in control.

I saw a poster with unforgettable words that I recalled all those years later. It said, "Smile; things could be worse. So I smiled, and they were." Four years before he died, John's digestive system basically stopped. Each of the drugs for emphysema caused constipation. So he took medications for constipation; everything he could find, he tried. Everything the doctors suggested, he tried. The years wore on, and finally nothing worked any more. It was a constant topic of conversation. I became so tired of the conversation, but I can only imagine how it must have been to be him!

On my sixtieth birthday, he had taken so much laxative that he experienced explosive diarrhea. It was a nightmare of epic proportions, and John cried like a baby. He felt sorry for himself, and I felt sorry for me. I wasn't happy to be turning sixty, and I was even more devastated to be living with a husband wearing diapers—his word, not mine. Buying them that first time was really tough.

That was his only day of self-pity. After that, he managed the laxatives. Our entire life was built around scheduling them and predicting when they would work. He might say, "I won't take them until tomorrow so that we can go to dinner tonight or church tomorrow." A miserable regimen, but a necessary one.

Toward the end came wheelchairs. Not being able to drive. Incredible weight loss. The hospital bed.

All very humbling. John accepted his new role. He made others feel loved, appreciated, important. The things he had learned in years past, he now served up as lessons, in generous doses, to anyone he came in contact with. These were lessons others learned by watching him. Meanwhile, John watched as his life seeped away slowly, day by day. I watched, too, and was amazed at his acceptance, with no complaints, of the freight train bearing down on him.

I think this is a perfect picture of what Scripture calls dying to one's self. John's biggest desire was—well, I can't honestly say, but from the outside it appeared to be serving others. He always had a big smile and an encouraging word. He laughed at your jokes and wanted to know how you were. No talk of his infirmities. He just wanted to talk about you and your accomplishments.

Toward the end, we installed a mechanical hospital bed in our bedroom. One night, he in his hospital bed, and me in our bed, he said, "How ya doin' over there."

I laughed and said, "I'm doing fine. How are you?" What a sweet moment.

John was true to himself until the end. My son marveled and had the perfect description for it. He said, "He's going to be John Pass to the very end!" In his last week of life, we went in to turn John—an every-two-hour duty. More humbling. Not to have the strength to move in the bed. Unfortunately, the result of not moving is bed sores, so it is necessary to be turned. John referred to my son and me as the Dream Team. One time, at about three o'clock in the morning, my son and I went in again to roll John over. He was fussing with his pajamas, which were all wrinkled up and disarranged around him. It was the first time John had complained about anything, and I didn't consider it a true complaint. But all of a sudden, his eyes got big and he said, "I'm getting grumpy." I laughed and said that he was never grumpy. His next statement blew me away. "I determined not to be."

I think of it now, that statement, and how John lay in that hospital bed and thought about how he wanted his last days on earth to be. He *decided* that he would live his life serving others, even if the only thing he could do was not grumble. He never so much as frowned again.

That humble man was not a beaten-down man, but a completed man.

To live is Christ, and to die is gain.

—Philippians 1:21

Jesus Loves Me

Isn't love grand? Songs are written about it. Poems. Books. Sonnets. Studies. What does it look like? Is it something you can "fall" into? And if so, can you "fall" out of it again? Is it always easy and fun? What happens when things get difficult?

John was a perfect example of what love looks like. John accepted all people for who they were—or even just who they said they were. Until you showed him something different, he believed who you said you were.

Even more importantly, when you failed and proved to be something less than advertised, he was the first to forgive and offer you another chance. John was married four times, and he had four families. (Not exactly a glowing example of marriage.) In each family there were children whom John took to be his own.

After his first marriage, whose details I do not pretend to know, his ex-wife moved to South America and took his first two biological children. He longed for relationship with those boys and grieved the loss. Far into his sixties, he attempted to reconnect with those children. He was rejected. For the first time, maybe in his life, he gave up. He had always had the boys in his will, which provided for a trust. He took them out. It was not that John was angered by rejection; rather, he accepted that they had another dad. A real dad. The dad who lived with them and loved them, taught them to play ball and shoot a gun. John fully understood that being a dad is not about biology; it is about love. And love is something you do. Something that thrives in the good times and grows rock strong when the times are tough.

John's second family stayed together for more than twenty-five years. He was married to a woman who had two children—a son, eight years old, and a daughter, thirteen. Then they added a third biological child, a daughter. He loved those children equally. When he spoke of his children, he made no distinction about their birth. When the son grew up and completed college, he desired to take John's last name. And so the son did. Few people realized that John's son was not a son by birth. They worked together as partners almost all of the son's adult life. When the son died suddenly at age sixty, John grieved deeply, as any other father would have done.

John also made no distinction about people's stations in life. John counted many powerful and successful people as his friends. John also befriended the clerks at grocery stores, cleaners, and various other establishments. The girl from the cleaners asked if she could visit in those last hospice months. The girls from the pharmacy came to his memorial service.

More significantly, John gave his time and attention to young people. A young woman came rushing up to me at the memorial service, sobbing, to tell me that John was the first person to make her feel welcome in church. I never knew. A seventeen-year-old woman from church came over in the last few days of John's life. She wanted to see him. I explained that he would not want visitors as he was now unresponsive. She asked if she could write a note that we could read to him. She wrote the dearest message, explaining how he had made her feel so special by keeping up with her athletic stats from the sports pages and complimenting her on them. Again, I never knew.

One of my favorite examples of the wide range of John's relationships was the janitor in the office complex where John worked. The man's name was Zack. At times in our dating years, I would meet John at his office and we would go for dinner, or maybe just a glass of wine, before we each headed home. We would encounter Zack in the hallways, beginning his cleaning. John would always stop and talk to Zack and inquire about his family and his horses.

I learned that Zack had taught John to rope. That was special because John owned roping horses, even a world championship horse, and employed trainers. Those trainers would have been honored to teach John to rope. John chose a janitor to teach him. No, John chose a friend.

My most favorite example of John's relatability was my children. My most favorite because, well, for obvious reasons. He treated both my children as he did his own—he considered them his own, not in a possessive sort of way, but in an appreciative, humble sort of way. He introduced them as his children. He provided like a father. He paid all their college expenses without question. John earned their respect—not because he provided, but because he loved. He taught them self-respect and character; he gave them a work ethic they still enjoy today. He embraced their friends—from grade school, from high school, from college, and after.

John showed his love in a godly way. The Bible says that we love because Jesus first loved us. I think John's experience of God's love was the source of John's love for others. Our church's definition of love is seeking the best for others, patiently, kindly, sacrificially, and unconditionally. John personified that kind of love.

> By this we know love, because He laid down His life for us. And we also ought to lay down our lives for the brethren.
>
> —1 John 3:16

A Man's Heart

The year between 12-12-11 and 12-12-12 was an unforgettable year. So many visions of John have taken up residence in my memories. The entire year was framed by the knowledge that each annual holiday or event likely would be a final one—last Christmas, last anniversary, last birthday. Yet I don't remember that time in a morose way. It was not a time of great sadness. It was a time of perseverance, putting one foot in front of the other. Perhaps, deep in the recesses of our souls, we each were coping with this reality in our own ways. Externally, we continued to live life.

For Christmas of 2011, we gave the grandchildren storybooks with recordings of John reading the stories in his wonderful voice. Each book had an integrated device that allowed for making voice recordings that would play as each page was turned. I knew what a treasure the recordings would be in the future. After Christmas, with the knowledge that John would more than likely not make it to another Christmas, I suggested that John record additional storybooks for all the adult children to be given the following Christmas.

In January 2012 we visited my son and his family. They were completing a building project, and the concrete was perfect for memorializing the tiny handprint of my grandson. Beside the handprint was a date: 1-21-12. Few things are literally set in stone, but that date is forever set in stone as the date of our last trip.

In March, I took a friend (ironically, a friend with another life-threatening disease, cancer) to the hill country to see the bluebonnets one final time. Like a journey to Mecca, the journey is a treasured tradition for many Texans to see the state flower in full bloom. To see the roadsides and hillsides awash in blue is a sight that endures in our hearts and calls us back year after year for a repeat performance. And the fragrance, oh, the fragrance.

We were only gone thirty-six hours, but it was the first time I had left John alone in several years. I phoned him many times throughout the day just to check on him—knowing he would be lonely. I had left him lots of food, and he had friends to call in the event of an emergency. He was fragile but not bedridden. I spoke with John several times on the second day—as we travelers meandered through the seas of blue and leisurely made our way back home. At about four o'clock that afternoon, we were still three hours away from home when I made another check-in call. I learned John was not feeling well. In fact, he had called in friends, who had spent the entire day with him. He had not told me in previous calls, because he did not want us to cut our trip short. I was apprehensive.

That was the longest three hours I had ever driven. I was not overly worried, just concerned. I needed to lay my eyes on him. I spoke with his "caregivers," who assured me that John was okay, maybe just missing me. I thought it was more than that. It was not in John's DNA to make a big deal of it—calling in the backup team and focusing attention on himself—unless he was significantly concerned.

Upon arriving home, again I was told by his friends that they thought John was just missing me. I had my doubts, but I couldn't see anything with my eyes. I determined that the next day I would get John to the doctor.

Aw, but when we got in bed, I knew. I could hear it. John had pneumonia. The gurgling sound was unmistakable. I had heard it so many times before.

I said let's go to the E.R. He said no; he was never going to the hospital again. I begged him. He declined. He was ready for hospice.

I didn't sleep all night. Between listening to him breathe and fearing the coming of dawn, I was so petrified. Praying. Praying. And additional praying. More like begging.

I was up early. Still praying. I had hardly slept at all; I was thinking of the implications of where we now found ourselves. At exactly 8:00 a.m., I called the hospice organization. They said they would send a nurse out to get us signed up. She would be there by 9:00 a.m.

I know it was a great shock to John to be awakened by me stating that the hospice nurse was there. My hurry was because I knew John needed antibiotics immediately if he had any chance at survival. Indeed, I didn't think oral antibiotics were powerful enough to do the trick. He was too compromised. He needed the strongest medicines available, administered intravenously. The hospice providers would only give him oral meds. That was better than nothing, I thought. After the nurse got him settled, she informed me, gently, that John might have two months to live.

Of course, she was wrong. We all were. God numbers our days, and He doesn't tell us the number. John lived for more than eight additional months.

***

John's memorial service was on December 18, 2012. My children left for their homes the following day. I committed to them that I would be following in three days to visit them. My mind was scattered, and I found it difficult to collect my thoughts enough to organize a trip. I was bouncing from one task to another. I went into John's closet. I found comfort in being with his things, and that's when I saw them. The storybooks. They were all stacked neatly on a shelf.

I sat down on the floor and opened them one by one. I heard the dedications, so sweet and heartfelt, in John's voice. A man who rarely expressed himself in flowery words had become a poet. He said such sweet and memorable things. His words wrapped me in a blanket of love. The dedication in my book ended with this thought: "And thank you for bringing me back to my faith, so that I can see you again." Indeed!

> As in water face reflects face, so a man's heart reflects the man.
>
> —Proverbs 27:19

No Jerks Allowed

It seemed unusual how young people wanted to hang out with someone sixty years their senior. But that is what happened. Our church hired a new worship leader and we took him to lunch. His name was Chris. He was about twenty-six years old, engaged, and an introvert. What could he possibly have in common with John?

You didn't really have to have something obvious in common with John to be his friend. John had taken a Dale Carnegie course when he was young and from it had developed a sincere gift in expressing his interest in people. He loved people of all ages, all interests, and all abilities. Before we arrived at any social gathering, John would drill me in the car on the way. He wanted to remember names of wives and children and any other pertinent facts. He wanted to be able to express his admiration for all their accomplishments. He wanted fond memories to be with him when he met old friends.

Then, as he spoke with someone, he looked the person straight in the eyes, never looking away, never spotting someone else more important. He concentrated on the one he was speaking with. Further, John would try to make a connection with that person. For example, if you were that person, maybe someone in your family went to Texas Christian University (go Frogs). Maybe you had lived in an apartment that he built. Maybe you liked horses. However long it took, John could find something in common with you. It was endearing to all who experienced it.

Chris, the worship leader, experienced this at full steam ahead. Chris had gone to school at Tarleton State in Stephenville, Texas. Bingo. We had owned a ranch in Stephenville! Instant connection.

Chris learned to relax around us. Chris liked to hang out with our small meeting group of older church members, which the pastor had dubbed The Old, the Rugged, and the Cross. Chris said he thought old people talked only about their health and the weather. That would not have been us! We laughed. A lot! Sometimes we attracted attention with our loud, joyful laughter. John's joyful, positive nature was contagious.

Chris had the opportunity to preach one Sunday. His emphasis was on getting to know lots of people—getting out of your comfort zone and meeting different people; becoming acquainted with people different from you. He used John as an example and said, "For instance, if you don't like John Pass, you're a jerk!"

An enduring slogan was born.

For Christmas that year, the "kids" from church (a/k/a our pastor and his wife and the worship leader and his wife) showed up with T-shirts for each of us. The shirts were black with white lettering. Three of the shirts said, "If you don't like John Pass you're a jerk." Mine said, "Sometimes I'm a jerk." (After all, I was married to him.) One said, "John Pass." And the final one said, "I'm a jerk." They were fun. We took pictures. The only problem was that Chris got the "I'm a jerk" shirt. He hated that because he was the one who had first come up with the phrase!

When John was in his last days, the pastor told John that he planned to wear his black T-shirt to do John's memorial service. Sure enough, the pastor showed up wearing the T-shirt under his dress shirt. And then he advertised, in accordance with the message of the T-shirt, that he was not a jerk.

It's true though. If you didn't like John Pass, you were a jerk! Everyone loved John Pass, and John Pass loved everyone!

> By this all will know that you are My disciples, if
> you have love for one another.
>
> —John 13:35

The Elephant in the Room

It was a beautiful day in July. John and I were sitting in the rocking chairs on our back porch. July in this part of the state, West Texas, can be mild or brutally hot. That particular day was mild. The back of the house overlooks a golf course; we could see many golfers taking advantage of the weather.

The porch is sheltered by a little nook in the back so that those sitting on the porch are in the shade. There is a wonderful fountain that pours over some stacked stones and falls four feet to make an incredibly soothing sound. Two ponds grace that hole of the course, attracting a plethora of birds. At various times of the year one can see Canadian geese, red-winged blackbirds, mockingbirds, egrets, great blue herons, orioles, purple martins, and a multiplicity of other birds. Once we even saw a giant pelican! Songs from some bird or other always fill the air. And unfortunately, often some profanities, as the golfers hate that hole—for the same reason the homeowners and the birds love it: the two ponds. Golfers call this water a hazard, but we think of the two ponds as an oasis in the desert.

On that particular day, John was recuperating from a stint in the hospital with pneumonia. The recovery wasn't going fast enough to suit John. The truth was that every bout of pneumonia left John's lungs just a little weaker. Each time he had pneumonia, it took longer to recover, and each time he lost a little lung capacity. So we sat there together on that day, rocking in our chairs, watching the birds and the golfers. We were taking it easy, each of us pensive.

John broke the silence. "Some nights I pray not to wake up the next morning."

Wow! How does one respond to such a statement? We both kept rocking as I considered what I would say. I knew that if I were in denial and dismissed the matter, assuring him that all would be okay, then it would shut him down. He needed to feel safe to say anything he wanted. If he thought I were flatly in denial or couldn't handle the topic, it would inhibit the process. After a few moments, I said, "I think I understand that. It's hard for me to hear, but I think I understand."

After a few more moments, John began to talk to me—about fear, death, dying, the challenges before him, and the challenges of just living each day, including literally taking one more breath.

A dam had burst. Up until that time, we had not spoken of his disease. Of the hopelessness of it. He had simply accepted the finality of the diagnosis, arisen each day, and faced it head on. I had wondered how he felt about it. I never asked questions at the doctor's office. I thought the questions of prognosis were questions for John to ask.

Now, he was telling me. Expressing those deep feelings of frustration that his body was failing him—not in the usual way that bodies wear out and age, but in a manner more distressing and fatal. How it felt to not have the energy (or breath) to just get ready to go out to dinner. Getting ready for church took him over two hours. It was a start and stop process. Begin and rest. Begin again and rest again, until the process was complete.

Next he began telling me things I needed to do when he was gone. I had no idea how invaluable these conversations would be to me. I would not have to wonder about what John would have done. He was telling me in advance! Our church is exceptionally good at assisting widows with all the decisions that have to be made, all the details about a life now gone. After John died, I had little need of that assistance, because John had helped me in advance; he had told me who I should talk to about different issues that would come up.

That first conversation lasted about thirty minutes, but it opened a door to an interesting period. We would just be driving down the street when John would say "I meant to tell you to keep the house" or comment on one of a million other tidbits that were important. Even as his body wore down, John's thoughts turned to me as he served the needs I did not yet know I had. And he was telling me at a time when I could ask questions.

After the initial thirty-minute conversation that day, we sat there in our rocking chairs, both lost in the thoughts of the mountain we had just scaled. About twenty minutes of silence passed before I looked over at him and said, "Do you want me to get the pillow?"

He burst out laughing and replied, "Not yet."

I had not meant it to be funny. I had said it to put a period at the end of the sentence so we could change the subject. Now there was nothing we couldn't talk about; the elephant had left the room.

> I consider that our present sufferings are not worth comparing with the glory that will be revealed in us.
>
> —Romans 8:18

Hero of the Faith

John was born into a Christian family. In relating the story of his life, he would begin with the fact they were at the church every time the doors opened—Sunday morning, Sunday night, Monday night visitation, and Wednesday night Bible study.

This devotion led to an overpowering moment when John was nine and felt God's call on his life. He said that he was unable to remain in the pew. It was as if he had no control over his legs. John went to the altar to declare his decision to follow Christ. John's call was strong. Eight years later, at age seventeen, he volunteered for service to fight in World War II. Unfortunately, when he left his family behind in Fort Worth, Texas, he also left his faith, or at least the practice of it. Sadly, John did not fulfill his desire to become a pilot; instead, he served his time in Puerto Rico with a team that repaired radios for planes coming out of combat.

After John came home from the war, a man now, no longer a boy, he attended Texas Christian University, paid for by the G.I. Bill. He received his degree in finance. John was brilliant with numbers. I heard a colleague say of John that he "could make the numbers dance." And so began his adult life, minus the practice of his faith.

From speaking with his children, I learned that there was a time in his life when he and his family attended church. Regretfully, when he moved his family to Dallas, once again he left his faith—or any participation—in West Texas with his former life.

In 1992, I became a believer and wanted to attend church. This was a time in our lives when things were terribly stressful for John and me. Not in our marriage, but in finances. Business failing. Bankruptcy. Searching for work. Searching for significance. John readily agreed to attend church with me. The first church we went to was the church where we had been married. We stayed there for a few months, but we didn't feel like we fit in—or perhaps we didn't want to fit in. The focus seemed to be more on how many people were there and what the mother-ship church was doing. We left for a church near us that placed more emphasis on the Bible; immediately we felt at home because we wanted to get to know God through His Word.

Thus began our growth in the knowledge of the Lord. We loved going to church together and soon began attending a Bible study. Within the first year, a friend invited us to another Bible study group—only problem was that it was forty-five minutes away. We went anyway. We loved the people: a firefighter, a businessman, a carpenter. People of diverse backgrounds, all trying to know God, understand His Word, and apply it to daily living.

The people in this group were so much fun—as well as knowledgeable in Scripture. We had prayer, Scripture study, dessert, and fun! I still recall some of the stories we exchanged, which John and I laughed about for years after we moved away. One of my favorites involved the time the leaders were taking a road trip. They stopped for dinner, and when Buzz got back into the car, he unbuttoned the top button of his jeans to be comfortable—not unusual for him. As they drove along in the dry Texas night, he asked his wife for Chapstick for his lips. She pulled a small tube out of her purse and he slathered the soothing substance on his lips as they continued along the way. Later, Buzz pulled into a service station to get gas. He went inside to get a cup of coffee. When he came out, he said, "Honey, why didn't you remind me to button my jeans. Those people were really looking at me funny!" Under the light of the gas pumps, she could now clearly see why they were staring. She had not given Buzz the Chapstick, but her lipstick! No wonder the people were looking at him funny!

After we moved to Midland, John continued to grow in his faith. He attended men's events at the church, including Bible studies with the pastor and other men. We also attended a weekly small group study that included wives. John became convicted that he had lived his life focused on the world rather than the Lord. His favorite song for a lot of years had been "I Did It My Way." A tune certain not to be on heaven's Top Ten playlist.

Oftentimes I hear believers fixate on their former lives—lives of sin. And while we all continue to sin, God has redeemed us. He has called us by name and forgiven our past. People who describe in great detail the sins of their past may appear to be bragging. Their constant public self-denigration begins to look like pride rather than humility. John was ashamed of his sinful past, but he accepted God's forgiveness and redemption. John would be first to say he had regrets, but he trusted what Christ had done for him; John preferred not to spend much time dwelling on or detailing his failures. Instead of focusing on his sin, John rested in God's grace. If you study the life of the apostle Paul, you will find that Paul never bragged about his past. Nor did he minimize or deny his past sin. Paul used his past as a lesson for the present.

The pastor at our home church in Midland gave a wonderful sermon one morning that he titled "Heroes of the Faith." First, he explained to us that a hero—whether a firefighter, soldier, or someone else—is almost always a person who denies having done anything special. A hero is a person who in the normal conducting of daily duties or daily life does what he or she is called to do. Our tendency as believers, no, as humans, is to desire to do something big and important. We want to be Billy Graham or Mother Teresa. And if we can't (and most of us can't), our inclination is to do nothing, or to undervalue the things we do to contribute. However, God recognizes our sincerity.

The pastor said that God sees us as heroes of the faith when we get up every morning and do the things set before us in our lives, whether changing diapers, digging ditches, or being a pastor. Our faithfulness is measured by how well we accomplish the tasks before us, whether large or small—not by how many souls were affected. It is important to perform God's work and calling in our lives, whatever that might be, remaining ever mindful that God can accomplish much with the smallest and weakest of us (such as Moses, David, Gideon, and others). That's how John lived his life.

In his last year, John's life was one of great suffering and sacrifice. It was a challenge just to get out of bed and walk to the kitchen. Actually, just to breathe. He never complained. When asked how he was, John gave quick answers and turned the topic to the other person. No need to grumble. He was a hero of the faith.

> I have fought the good fight, I have finished the race, I have kept the faith.
>
> —2 Timothy 4:7

31

Just Do It

John was always serving. All through our marriage, he served me. He was always doing something. If John saw anything that needed to be done, he just did it. He never pointed out that it needed to be done. He never asked someone else to do it. John personified the Nike slogan "Just do it."

John's mother died at age eighty-nine when John was sixty-three. John had provided for his mother since she retired at sixty-five, and really many years before that. John's father had been a firefighter and died at age forty-nine. John had been his mother's main source of support ever since. "Meme" had worked at a department store until she retired, but John had provided housing and extras in those years. Not only that—he also called his mother daily to check on her and pay attention to her. He never complained. John loved Meme, and he showed it by his service to her.

Before my children left home for college, a nickname they gave to John was Bowl Patrol. John was always on the lookout for any glass or bowl that was empty or nearly empty and sitting on a table somewhere. Only problem was that there might be one last sip or one last bite remaining. It was not too unusual to hear "What happened to my Dr. Pepper? Big Sir, I wasn't finished with that!"

A young man, Jeff, from our church, who loved to spend time with John, tells the story about John once advising him to always make certain there were no dirty dishes left in the sink before he went to bed at night. It was just a small thing about serving one's wife—something that would make her morning better. John did not even remember saying it, but Jeff never forgot. He put it into practice in his life. Jeff's father observed him putting dishes away and questioned him. The man laughed at the simplicity—as if such a small act would have much effect.

After some consideration, Jeff's father decided to implement the small change in his own life. When asked about it, his wife of more than thirty years just smiled coyly.

The benefit of serving one another is often overlooked in our culture of "Me! Me! Me!" The reality is that service to the important people in your life is *not* demeaning. Being served by another is very endearing. One result can be the beginning of a spirit of reciprocity, but even if your service goes unthanked or unnoticed, the worst result could be that your own heart is changed!

One thing John always did was to open my car door when we were getting into the car. In those last years, when he had little breath, I asked him not to do it. I knew it was difficult for him to forgo, but his breath and his energy had to be conserved. One time when my children were visiting, John asked Shayne to get my door. The way John phrased it made us all laugh. He said, "Shayne, you get Mom's door and I'll get mine." Say what?

In the last few months of his life, John could do little for himself. He hated that, probably as much as he hated being sick. He said to me one day, "I hate that you have to do everything for me." I reminded him that he had served me all his life and it was now my time to return the favor.

The Son of Man did not come to be served, but to serve.

—Matthew 20:28

Sweet Spirit

The last thing I expected was the sweetness. My perception had always been that death is harsh. When John's death came, it was anything but harsh. So many memories of that time flash through my mind's eye, and each time they still bring a sweetness, a gentleness, a smile—and a tear.

My son rushed to Midland when I called to tell him that the hospice nurse had said that John would be in heaven for Christmas. The date of the call was November 26. My son wanted to spend all the time he could with John. Unfortunately, my daughter had two pretty small children, and one can't just get a sitter and leave a two-year-old and a four-year-old—not easily anyway—so my daughter followed a few days later on December 2.

On Tuesday night we had a party. Really, we did. It was an impromptu party. People just showed up spontaneously. The worship leader brought his guitar and his sweet wife, and they sang songs—some of the songs they would later sing at John's memorial service. It was a joyous time with people laughing and telling stories and John being right in the thick of things. Begging for one more song.

Singing along with what breath he had. There were thirteen people in that room—along with a king-size bed and his hospital bed.

All the company didn't leave until nearly eight-thirty that evening. A dear friend had brought over a gourmet dinner ready to cook. I put it in the oven. My son and daughter opened a bottle of wine. John hinted that he wanted a glass, but I thought better of it—mixing alcohol and morphine didn't seem like a wise decision. I doubt that decision now wondering what real difference it could have made.

The four of us ate our dinner in the bedroom—Christi and I sitting on the king bed, Shayne in a chair, and John in his hospital bed. John had a tiny bit of salmon and a bite of a roll. We sat there and relived other dinners—in better times. It was anything but melancholy. It was just another family dinner under different circumstances.

The next day, out of earshot of my children, I said to John that I was secretly glad that it had been only the four of us—back to how we were in the beginning of our life together. I love my sweet daughter-in-law and son-in-law, but it was a great bookend for our life—this last time with only us four. I wouldn't have said it to my children; but later that day, at separate times, both of my children came to me and said how glad they were that it had been only the four of us. Sweet.

Every morning I would text about thirty people who were keeping up with us—praying for us, loving on us. One morning I opined that I felt like the mashed potatoes of life, and they were all the gravy. A few days later a jar of gravy appeared on my doorstep. Sweet.

A friend made five pounds of fudge and brought it over. Every time I looked up, one of us was eating a piece of fudge. My daughter had to go home after only a few days, but when we got down to the last few pieces of fudge, we saved them for her—knowing the time was short until she returned. Fudge, oh so sweet!

I can only guess how difficult it was for Christi, our daughter, to leave with full knowledge that it would be her last time to see Big Sir on this earth. She went home and made it her mission to send us videos of her babies singing and performing—one every hour. Those videos helped us so much. They gave us something to smile about. Something to change the subject. Something to look forward to. Something so sweet.

There was a friend who came by at about seven-thirty nearly every morning. He would sit on the edge of John's bed. He would refer to John as John Boy and inquire what we needed for the day. Did we have lunch? Dinner? He still came after John was nonresponsive. This friend would go in, give John a little pat, and then sit in the living room with my son and me and go over our day. On the Sunday before John died, we asked for people to come and sit with us. We didn't really want to be alone when John left this life. Accordingly, through the day, men came in four-hour shifts and sat with us. They talked about football, college days, and other things to take our minds off our reality. Very sweet.

A young man came and brought a six-pack of beer; he sat with my son. They drank a couple of beers and talked about football, beer, and life. Sweet.

There was a cloud that settled over our home, a cloud of sweetness. Like a hug from God. It warmed us and took us through the time of waiting for death. John died on a Wednesday. It was not harsh.

> O Death, where is your sting
> O Hades, where is your victory?
>
> —1 Corinthians 15:55

Just Like He Said

For almost a decade (I hope I'm not exaggerating) John was in charge of preparing the bread and wine for communion at our church. He inherited the job from someone who moved away. The communion ceremony occurred on the first Sunday of each month, and John loved preparing for it. This was a responsibility he took very seriously.

On Friday he would check the supplies and see what was lacking. Then, when necessary, he would go to the grocery store to get grape juice and to the Christian bookstore for bread or the cups in which communion was served.

On Saturday afternoon John would go to the church and meticulously put everything together for Sunday morning.

One Sunday morning, John had made everything ready as usual— well, almost everything. After the bread was served, prayed over, and consumed by the congregation, there was a visible reaction going through the people. Something was amiss. It turned out that when John had gone to the bookstore, the communion bread that he usually purchased had been sold out. With no other option, he had purchased the squishy bread rather than the crunchy bread. As we sat there, a ripple went thru the crowd. John and I both looked toward the pastor, who was looking back at John with a sly grin. We both knew John was in for some serious razzing.

We were right. After communion, the pastor returned to the pulpit and questioned aloud whether John had purchased day-old communion bread. Periodically, the teasing would resurface. It was fun to tease John because he took it so well.

John continued to prepare for communion, even as he lost his strength. So we began preparing for communion as a team. About a year later, a couple of guys who really loved John began helping him with these communion tasks. They made an event out of it by having lunch on Saturday afternoon before going to the church to prepare. John really looked forward to spending time with those men, and he loved being able to continue his service.

Once, when John had been in the hospital and was feeling weak and terrible, I suggested that perhaps it was time for him to step down from his communion duties. His reply was "I'll do it as long as I am able." Obviously, I thought that the time when he could no longer do this had arrived, but I was wrong.

After John died, I was in the Christian bookstore. The checkout clerk looked at the name on my credit card and asked if I knew John Pass. Having difficulty voicing the words, I finally said that he was my husband, but that he had gone to glory. She remembered him— his years of purchasing supplies once a month.

John persevered. He continued preparing for monthly communion until he began hospice care. Now that I think about it, he did it until he was no longer able, just like he said.

> We also glory in tribulations, knowing that tribulation produces perseverance, and perseverance, character, and character hope. Now hope does

not disappoint, because the love of God has been poured out in our hearts by the Holy Spirit which was given to us.

—Romans 5:3–4

All Labor Is Profitable

John loved to work. Really. He had several careers in his lifetime. He began as a salesman out of college. He was a natural. He traveled all over West Texas selling bandages and first aid supplies to drug stores. John was diligent. He worked hard. He was dependable. He strove to deliver whatever he promised. His word was his contract.

Even though John was a natural salesman, in his early twenties he took a Dale Carnegie course to enhance his sales skills. He was always striving to be the best he could be. Dale Carnegie taught leadership training and sales techniques long before such training was popular. Mr. Carnegie died in 1955, but his courses are still taught. His most famous book was *How to Win Friends and Influence People.* A few memorable quotes from his writing are as follows:

- Success is getting what you want. Happiness is wanting what you get. (Carnegie, Matching Quotes by Dale Carnegie 2015)
- Don't be afraid to give your best to what seemingly are small jobs. Every time you conquer one it makes you stronger. If you do the little jobs, the big ones tend to take care of

themselves. (Carnegie, Matching Quotes by Dale Carnegie 2015)

- The successful man will profit from his mistakes and try again in a different way. (Carnegie, Matching Quotes by Dale Carnegie 2015)
- Always make the other person feel important. (Carnegie, How to Win Friends and Influence People 1936)106
- Remember that a person's name is to that person the sweetest and most important sound in any language. (Carnegie, How to Win Friends and Influence People 1936)118

I watched John "work" that course all his life: remembering people's names, making a connection, making people feel important. Looking at it now, I wonder if John learned those ideas from Dale Carnegie or whether they were innate qualities of John's character.

At some point in his late twenties, John went to work selling homes for a builder. He was extremely successful. He learned all he could about construction, all the while honing his skills as a salesman.

Next, John partnered with another man in the construction business, and they began building homes. Then they went on to the development of entire communities, which meant laying out the streets, bringing in water and electricity. They soon decided their future was in building apartments. John eventually opened his own company and built more than thirteen thousand apartment units.

After twenty-five years and a serious downturn in the market, John was really fumbling for something to do. For a while, he went back into sales—selling apartment projects. But after about five years, he joined his son in a fast food venture, which grew into a rather large business. Hard work and success were a part of most things John did.

All through the years, I continued to see John work his Dale Carnegie course. John became the consummate negotiator. He never gave up. His goal was for everyone to walk away from the table happy. He always focused on the positive—working hard to eliminate the negative so that everyone could walk away truly satisfied.

John was terrified of retirement. After John sold his share of the fast food business, he stayed on for a few years, but eventually the new owners moved the offices out of Midland. John was out of a job.

His worst fear was becoming a reality. Then, he struck up a friendship with a neighbor who had a successful business. The next thing I knew, John was an official *kinda-sorta* consultant attending their executive meetings. John had been so very worried that he was going to be put out to pasture. This man looked at John and saw his wisdom where others only saw his age. When I see that dear neighbor, he still never fails to tell me how valuable John was and how they still miss him.

Wherever John worked, he focused on several elements—doing an excellent job, being totally loyal to his employer, and making his working environment pleasant for those around him. Always practicing that Dale Carnegie course, he got to know people, made friends, and helped others enjoy their work. Did he do that to get something for himself? Almost everything John did was to enhance the lives of those he came into contact with. And in the process, his life was most certainly better.

Through the years, all of us in the family found ourselves focusing on John's work. If we were traveling, we might be looking at apartment projects in other cities. When he was in the restaurant business, I ate way more burgers than I ever thought I wanted. When we visited a drive-through restaurant, we always had to time how long the order took, see if the signs and parking lots were well lit, and assess whether everything was clean and everyone courteous. We even had to count the catsup and napkins. When he acted as a consultant, we spent lots of time looking at gas stations and convenience stores: checking prices, cleanliness, and friendliness.

Details. Always looking at the details. John had an incredible gift for the details in life and for loyalty. If we were eating fast food, we chose to eat at his establishment. If we were buying gas, it was from his friend. We didn't get any special treatment at either of those businesses. John felt he owed them his business. In the big picture, does it matter so much where one individual bought his burgers or his gasoline? I think it does. Those qualities embodied the integrity of the man. John lived his beliefs every day.

Many times I witnessed the result of John's attitude about work and its effects on those around him. To the people working for him, and his peers working with him, John brought a joy in his work which was contagious. His attitude changed the environment.

There are many proverbs in Scripture about work. The labor of the righteous leads to life. All labor is profitable. In the book of Ecclesiastes, Solomon asked the question, "What profit has a man from all his labor." His answer is one John exemplified in his life and his love of work:

> For my heart rejoiced in all my labor;
> And this was my reward for all my labor.

> —Ecclesiastes 2:10

A Good Name Is
Better than Riches

John had great integrity. Only once in our life together did I ever see anyone challenge John's integrity. And it was a doozy.

In the late 1980s, after the real estate market crashed, there were many developers investigated, indicted, and sent to prison for their activities that crossed the line. Land and property had been flipped, again and again. (A flip refers to a transaction that is made with no intention of actually moving into or operating the property. The purchase is made solely to increase the value before remarketing the property and selling ("flipping") it for a considerable profit.) A single piece of property might quadruple in months. Investigators were looking into appraisers and bankers along with developers and speculators. Lenders and appraisers were being accused of taking money under the table, i.e., bribes, in order to make the transactions happen.

One day John came home from work looking particularly stressed, his tie askew, shoulders slumping, and little color in his face. After he removed his suit jacket, we sat down to talk. John told me he had been visited by federal investigators. From their questions it seemed that their focus was a lender John had used frequently to finance apartment projects. The investigators accused John of kickbacks, payoffs, and other criminal activity. They demanded reams of documentation to prove his innocence. John had spent hours with these men while they accused and excoriated him, everything but flogging! And they promised to return until they got what they wanted from him.

John was afraid. I was afraid. I asked him if he had done anything to worry about. His reply was firm: "No, I never participated in anything I felt was not above board. It has been too easy to make money legally. It would have been pure greed to cheat!" Later, months later, at an outing with friends, other developers, John and the guys determined that controlled greed was a good thing. Controlled greed was simply ambition. In contrast, we could all see the results of uncontrolled greed. Uncontrolled greed had led good people to lose their moral compass and commit crimes that they might not have committed otherwise. The legitimate, ambitious businesspeople worked hard and made smart decisions, while not letting money be the sole focus. When money is the only goal, it is easy to find ways to make money that are less than honorable.

The investigators clamored for more and more information, unrelenting in their demands. John and his office staff spent hours and days providing mountains of reports to establish paper trails of transactions.

During this time, John came home with tales of other developers facing investigations. A domino effect ensued. Each day's news brought reports of people indicted. People we knew, some well.

Once, we were in Santa Fe, New Mexico, for a brief holiday when a strange thing happened. John saw a developer he knew and waved at him across the courtyard. The guy actually ducked behind a column! John assumed that the guy was either embarrassed or didn't want to be seen! No one knew who was talking to the feds, and if you were in a compromised position, you were probably paranoid! That developer later served time in Club Fed, as the federal prison for white-collar crime is tagged.

Many others did not go to prison. We heard stories of people who "hid their money in a coffee can. What might be termed the talk around the water cooler was that many people in the real estate field had done shady deals. It is likely that some people were hiding money from lenders rather than paying on the loans. We could also see that there were many developers who were like John and not hiding money. Those people were suffering. As a result of the real estate market crash, John was deep in debt. He joked about the coffee can, but he never seriously considered it as an option. He knew he owed the money. John was honest, and he paid as long as possible and then did the unthinkable: he declared bankruptcy. That, too, was an interesting situation because by the time John went into bankruptcy, the only remaining bank to whom John owed money had been dissolved— leaving him no options for negotiating payment.

What John did not do was compromise his ethics. Sure, he hated what was happening to us. Sure, he wished it was different. In the end, the federal investigators went away. They saw no wrongdoing on John's part—he did not cut corners, take kickbacks, pay bribes, fail to report earnings to the IRS, or commit any other illegal activity. He hated it when he declared bankruptcy. He was ashamed, but not beaten.

John recovered. It took many years. His dear son offered him an opportunity to join him in a fast food business venture. John was seventy years old at that time, but his mind remained sharp. John worried that he would not be an asset. He knew nothing of the fast food business. John did not want charity.

John's first assignment was to look at each check before it was mailed. He came home at the end of the first week and declared with a big smile that he had made his salary for the month. Naturally, I inquired how he had done that. John, who had a keen eye for detail, had found enough monetary errors to equal his salary for a month—in the first week! He knew he had a place in the company.

That was the beginning of a new career. John grew as the business grew. Eventually the company owned ninety stores.

Harry Truman said, "Fame is a vapor, popularity is an accident, riches take wings, those who cheer today may curse tomorrow and only one thing endures—character." (Truman 2015)

John could have been in jail. Some were. His character kept him from that destiny. John's character and good name went with him to the grave.

> A good name is to be chosen rather than great riches, Loving favor rather silver and gold.
>
> —Proverbs 22:1

Pie Oh My

John was a lot like Will Rogers, but as always, John was just a little different! John never saw a piece of pie he didn't like! I've never been very good at making pies, but I would make them periodically using premade crusts. One year at Christmastime, I gave John a gift certificate to the Pie of the Month Club. John was in heaven! In all our thirty-five years, I had never received such an enthusiastic response to a gift! Holy macaroni, he was thrilled just studying the brochure. John made his culinary plans by the month for the entire year!

First came an apple pie—best we'd ever eaten—with caramel sauce. John had his with vanilla ice cream. Next came the pecan (again, enjoyed with ice cream). I can't remember what came next, but it was just as wonderful. The next thing that occurred was just plain shocking. The pie company said it would no longer send pies. It cancelled the balance of the contract and refunded the difference. *No!* Not his all-time favorite gift! But yes, it was over.

There would be no more pie. Done. Finished. Kaput.

Up stepped Jenny. She rode in on her white horse, rolling pin in hand. Jenny was twenty-six and wife of the worship leader, Chris, at our church. Jenny sang like God's prettiest songbird, and boy, could she make pie! We met Jenny when Chris came to the church and they were only engaged. New to the area, alone in West Texas, an entirely new world, the two of them became fast friends with John and me. We enjoyed lunch after church every Sunday. I was Jenny's mentor, and the two of us had lunch occasionally. It was a special relationship.

Being a stand-up friend and a huge fan of Big Sir, Jenny offered to pick up where the offending company had left off. She inquired of John what type of pie he would like. The reply came after some thought—strawberry. Young and sweet, Jenny wasn't assertive enough to say that she didn't make strawberry. Instead of saying "Choose again!" she set about looking for a recipe. She found a number of them in her cookbooks and online. After some experimentation, Jenny developed her own recipe by combining recipes. And *voilà*, strawberry pie!

And was it good. Mmmm, so very good.

Since Jenny's pies were such a hit with John, Jenny decided she could raise Christmas money by offering her own Pie of the Month Club to some of her friends. I signed up, as did a number of others from the church.

Those monthly pies were heaven. We sometimes shared with friends and family; sometimes we hoarded them for ourselves. It was such a pleasure to see Jenny pull up with the treasure of the month!

Alas, I could see it was unlikely that John would live to see his twelve months of pies. After I called to relay the message that John would be in heaven for Christmas, Jenny cried all day as she made his last pie. Her sweet son, Blane (a/k/a the Little Red-Headed Buddy of Big Sir), asked why she was crying. Jenny replied, "Big Sir is going to heaven to see Jesus."

Blane's immediate response was "I want to go to heaven and see Jesus!"

Jenny's last gift to Big Sir was not the pie. Jenny's last gift was the clear, sweet singing she provided with such joy at Big Sir's home-going celebration.

Taste and see that The Lord is good.

—Psalm 34:8

What Goes Around

I called John a pied piper. He was a friend magnet. Careful consideration reminds me of what it was like to live with him—a small example of living with a rock star. In 2008 when John had his first bout with pneumonia, we were inundated with visitors at the hospital.

Each episode of pneumonia brought a seven- to ten-day stay in the hospital. This first episode was quite alarming to his friends—to all of us. That first seven-day stay in the hospital brought fifty visitors. My son kept saying to me, "Mom, he doesn't need all this company. He can't get any rest." I never considered asking people not to come. I knew John so well. He got better much quicker with all the company. I can still see the faces of those visitors.

There were many hospital stays. Each time there were men who came. The last time John went to the hospital was in late October 2011, a stay that would last two weeks. When he woke up that morning at home, I knew John had pneumonia. He was extremely weak. I also knew that I, personally, could not get him into the car to go to the hospital. He knew I was considering calling the paramedics. He asked me earnestly not to make him go in an ambulance.

How could I not honor that simple request? Such a small thing. I called our elder, Vince, and asked if he could come and help me. He said that he would be right over. On his way, he obviously called the church and gave a request for the prayer chain. When we got to the hospital, there was already a young man there waiting for us.

We arrived about noon and were in the emergency room until 5:00 p.m. We had more than twenty guests that afternoon. And the stream continued for two weeks. Visitors. Often they brought meals, so that we were both quite well fed. One evening, a couple brought dinner and stayed to eat with us. Just what the doctor ordered.

One night in June 2012, some guys who like to "pick and grin" came over, played instruments, and sang for two hours. John was delighted.

In July some friends from church invited eighty people over to our house one evening. It was, for all practical purposes, an opportunity to say good-bye. We had already been housebound for over three months. These people came in with food, paper plates, and everything they needed to throw a party. When it was over, they cleaned up and took the trash with them. Nothing remained but the joy of the party.

And then there was the Thursday night dinner gang. They came each week, bringing dinner and laughter. They were young. Loud and funny. They, too, brought dinner and cleaned up. When they left, we were exhausted from all the energy after so much solitude.

John would say to me, "What were they laughing about?"

I would say, "I have no idea!" Such joy.

Looking back, I realize that few of those visitors realized the service they provided. And I would guess that many were just returning the love John had given them in years past.

> And just as you want men to do to you, do to them likewise.
>
> —Luke 6:31

I've Got the Joy, Joy, Joy

As I said earlier, John was the pied piper of men, young and old. They wanted to talk to him, absorb his spirit, pick his brain, be like him. I saw it throughout our years together. The junior partners at the law firm. The young men at church. The young men in his office. The friends of my son. Those last few years, I called it the Float Fellowship. There was always some young man on our back porch having a root beer float with John. He asked me one day, "Why do they come here for a root beer float? They could get one anywhere." I replied that I thought they came to be with him.

He thought about it for a moment and said, "No, I don't think that's it."

As he became sicker, I would occasionally call the elders, and a few of them would come over and pray for him. It made us both feel better. We noticed that after they prayed they would mill around outside for a while. We never knew why. After John was gone, one of the elders told me that the group of elders would stand in the front yard, astonished that while they had come over to encourage John, he had given them encouragement.

The last nine months of his life, John was under hospice care and almost totally confined to home. One Sunday, we ventured out to church. It was quite a struggle, but we both really wanted to go. When we pulled up into the handicapped parking, several men ran over to get John's wheelchair out and help him into it. They sent me on my way, insisting that they had it covered. I went inside and was visiting with my friends when a hush fell over the lobby. I turned to see what it was. And it was John. Men were moving quietly toward the door to shake his hand. He was a celebrity!

That was how it was until the end. Men coming and hanging out, sitting on the corner of the hospital bed we had moved into our bedroom. Laughter ringing in the rooms and forever in our hearts.

These things I have spoken to you that my love may
remain in you, and that your joy may be complete.

—John 15:11

Like Father, Like Son

John and J.T. They were like brothers, friends, or buddies. J.T. came into John's life when J.T. was only eight years old and John married his mother. The story John told me was that J.T. was quite shy in those days and pretty beaten down from his first eight years of life. John could still recall how the shoulders of J.T. slumped in defeat. Somewhere along the way that changed. Love has a way of healing us of the hurts we suffer.

John related stories of J.T. hanging out at job sites as a young boy and eventually working in the construction business. And stories of playing basketball in high school. Then, there were the stories of life at Texas Christian University when J.T. had chosen John's alma mater—much to John's delight! When J.T. graduated from TCU, he legally changed his last name to Pass and joined John Pass Investments. In short order, John made J.T. a junior partner. They worked hard.

It is fun to recall the memories of them together—they were a good team and they bought ranches about half an hour apart, southwest of Fort Worth, in the early '80s. Most weekends were spent at the ranch, and we saw J.T. and his family at least once through the weekend. John and J.T. spoke on the phone often, sometimes about business and sometimes about ranches and cattle. They went into the cattle business together, importing the first Chianina cattle from Italy. Chianina were large, very large, white cows that produced extremely lean meat. The Pass Cattle Company bred them with Black Angus cattle to produce black cows that were more pleasing in color to the judges at cattle shows. John and J.T. once had a bull named Boxcar (for obvious reasons). They also had a beautiful heifer, Velvet (her black coat looked like velvet), who won the national championship in Louisville, Kentucky. Partners in everything. Those were the days of boots and belts, big hats, big parties, and big fun.

J.T. did not look at all like John. John was six feet tall, but J.T. was well over six feet, with sandy brown hair and a thin build. Both were handsome. But it wasn't J.T.'s looks that drew people to him. Just as with John, J.T.'s charm was practically irresistible.

J.T. was like the kid in high school who was so much fun that everyone pushed to sit next to him to be close to the action. J.T. had John's personality—or maybe John's personality on steroids. J.T.'s charisma filled a room with energy and enthusiasm. He worked hard and played hard. And he loved John.

One of the most poignant events that I remember occurred a few years prior to J.T.'s untimely death. We received a call early one Sunday morning that J.T. was in the hospital and had perhaps suffered a heart attack. We left immediately for Fort Worth. The four-hour drive was quiet, both of us lost in our thoughts. We finally arrived, exhausted. When we walked into the hospital room, J.T. began to cry. The sight of his dad was just too much. They both shed tears—tears of fear, tears of joy, tears of love, and tears of gratitude.

J.T., like his father, had a great faith in God. And like his father, it was a faith J.T. left at one point to focus on the world, and a faith to which he returned. When he came back to his faith, J.T. did faith like he did life—full speed ahead, all out or all in. Often J.T. would call John with spiritual or scriptural questions. J.T. had a zeal for God's Word and spent many hours reading, studying, and thinking.

My biggest takeaway from J.T.'s life is that he remained the same fun person after he came back to his faith. While he changed some of his activities, he remained the magnetic man he had always been. (This should speak to anyone who is hesitant to commit to the Lord, thinking that it would mean giving up having fun!) In his last years, J.T. liked to say that a perfect day for him was sitting on the dock with friends, fishing and talking about God.

The entire family celebrated John's seventy-fifth birthday at J.T.'s home—children, grandchildren, and all the spouses, about twenty people in total. We ate together, had our pictures made, one last time, and stayed up half the night laughing and telling stories. As we ate our last sandwich on Sunday prior to loading into cars to go separate directions, J.T. began to talk about what fun it would be to be raptured to heaven right then! He was right, too. There was much pain in the future of our family, and I for one would have been delighted to be raptured that day!

J.T.'s life was cut short at the age of sixty by heart disease. Two and a half weeks before John's eightieth birthday, we received the call at 4:45 a.m. The call you never want to receive—the call that sucks the wind from the room. John was inconsolable. He felt that somehow he should have done something! Surely a father is not supposed to outlive his son.

After J.T.'s death, I witnessed a number of times when John would pick up the phone to begin making a call and then put the phone back down again with a quizzical look on his face. I knew that he had started to call his beloved son to share some tidbit of the day. This was a foreshadowing of things to come in my own life—wanting to share something with John, only to realize that it was no longer possible.

At least John and J.T. are together. Partners again. Now, they look alike. Now they look like their heavenly Father.

> Beloved, now we are children of God; and it has not yet been revealed what we shall be, but we know that when He is revealed, we shall be like Him, for we shall see Him as He is.

> —1 John 3:2

The Law

The boys were only about fourteen, so they were definitely enjoying the ride—and what a ride it was! John had a new car with a big engine, and he had decided to see exactly what the car would do. We were just leaving the ranch on a Sunday afternoon, John and I, Shayne and his friend Chuck. The race track was just a long straight road with no other cars in sight—so John put the pedal to the metal and off we went. The boys were literally pinned back against the back seat, giggling with glee and urging John on: "Go, Big Sir!"

As it turns out, we were *not* the only car on the road. Suddenly, John took his foot off the accelerator and declared, "Oh, no!"

Yep, it was a state trooper. I didn't feel very sorry for John, because I was the sole sane voice in the car—also known as the wet blanket. "Oh, Mom," Shayne had said, "he's just having fun."

John pulled over and began the process of getting his license from his wallet. The boys were still giggling and I was waiting smugly when the trooper came to the window and leaned down to speak to John. "What's the hurry— Oh, I'm sorry, Mr. Pass. I didn't recognize you. How ya doin'?"

"If it was any better I couldn't stand it! Haven't seen you in a while," John said.

"No, I've been working a different area lately. Things okay at the ranch?"

And so it went. John almost always had a heavy foot, but rarely got caught. Here he had been caught, but it was obvious he was going to be let off! The boys loved it. They were not getting the lesson I had thought they would get, the one I thought they needed. In fact they got exactly the opposite lesson, and I fumed a bit.

To redeem himself, John looked up into the rearview mirror and said, "Don't drive like this, kids." They roared in laughter. I winced; once again I had become the ogre and John the good guy. I would never learn.

John's philosophy of parenting was often to make the kids laugh. Looking back, I have to admit that it worked pretty well most of the time. I can also say that in life, it is better, almost all the time, to laugh rather than cry. John and I laughed through most of the hard times we endured together. There's always something to laugh about, and the more we laugh at ourselves, the easier life is. Life can be serious, difficult, and just plain hard. Our ability to see the lighter side helps us to take ourselves less seriously. To laugh helps us to remember that individually, we are of little consequence in this world. I like to describe myself as a flea bite on the ankle of life.

Interestingly, the self-denigration reminds me not only of how small and unimportant I am in the big picture of life, but also how humbling it is to have the love of the Creator of this wonderful universe we live in. We are small and inconsequential—and yet treasured by God and made to be a piece of a puzzle so intricate that only He could have designed it! Not only do I have the love of God to buffer me against the harshness of the world, but also He created me with a job to do, which only I could accomplish.

More than twenty years later, John and I were driving down another isolated road. This time John was driving seventy, which was the speed limit, or so he thought. When he saw the flashing red lights in his rearview mirror, John complained, "I can't believe he is going to stop me. I was not speeding."

The trooper was very young. He looked as if he couldn't be any older than a teenager! His ears stuck out and balanced his large cowboy hat to keep it from falling into his eyes. He took John's license and went back to his car to check whether John had any outstanding arrest warrants.

When the young trooper returned, he leaned against our car and explained to John that the speed limit was reduced to sixty for about a mile. Then he said something surprising: "Mr. Pass, were you *really* born in 1926?"

Once again John did not receive a traffic ticket, and once again we laughed.

> For the law of the Spirit of life in Christ Jesus has made me free from the law of sin and death.
>
> —Romans 8:2

John and Diann

JT and John

John and Sissy

John and Christi

SHAYNE AND JOHN

JOHN AND DIANN

Kendall John Kristin Alison

JOHN AND CINDY

Not Any Old Joe

John had a gentle spirit. He was sensitive to the feelings of other people. A sweet story was told to me by one of his friends after his death. This was a man near fifty years old who, as a younger man, had come to our church when he had moved to Midland. Eventually he had joined a men's Bible study that the pastor held during lunch on Wednesdays. This study group stayed together for several years—it may still be going on—but John attended for about a decade.

The group was diverse: young, old, executives, Bible scholars, and novices. They had a rule that what happens at Bible study stays at Bible study—the Las Vegas rule. So I didn't—still don't—know what was discussed.

Except for this one story.

This young man had not grown up in our church, and he didn't have the same Bible knowledge that many of the men in the group had. He told me that initially he didn't even take his Bible to the study, because he didn't know how to find anything in it. He felt so uncomfortable, but he enjoyed the study and the fellowship with the other men. So he pressed on.

John made many strong friendships in that Wednesday lunch study group, including his friendship with this young man, Joe. Joe told me how he would always sit beside John because John would shift his Bible slightly over so that Joe could see it. Joe never asked John to do that, but John obviously sensed Joe's discomfort about his inability to locate particular books in the Bible in a timely manner.

Such a small way to serve. It may seem insignificant, but it was quite memorable to Joe, the beneficiary of John's largesse. Sometimes the smallest acts can make the biggest difference! Today's world is enamored by random acts of kindness. These are often things like discreetly paying for someone's coffee or lunch. Those are certainly acts to be commended. However, there are many ways to touch a life by just being simply attuned to the needs of others. John had an acute awareness of ways to serve others.

Joe still attends our church. I see him most Sundays sitting with his precious wife and listening intently. I smile to know that my husband was able to give confidence to a younger man struggling and trying to fit in. I feel confident that Joe will, in his lifetime, reach out the hand of friendship to other struggling young men.

Be kindly affectionate to one another with brotherly love, in honor giving preference to one another.

—Romans 12:9

Gotcha, Mr. Pass

One of the fun things John and I did for several years was to take our pastor and his wife to dinner, along with the worship leader and his wife. John liked to take them to eat a big steak. They were all young, and it was a real treat for them to go somewhere nice and choose anything from the menu without regard to the cost. It was a real cholesterol bonanza!

We loved these young people. We always included them in birthday and holiday celebrations. They never said no. And they became, really, part of the family.

One October we took the two couples out. We were seated, and our favorite waiter came bounding up to the table. He enthusiastically said, "Whiskey, Mr. Pass?" John obviously was appalled. Here, before the pastor and worship leader, he had been outed as one who appreciated whiskey! Our four guests looked amused. John began to stammer, and the more he stammered, the more they laughed. It is not like he was a closet drunk or something. He was accustomed to having a drink when we went out to dinner—not a six-pack or a bottle of wine, but a drink. The truth is that in earlier days, John had been more of an imbiber, but those days were long gone. Now, here he sat trying to explain a single drink.

The "kids," as we called them, didn't let us forget. This moment became one of those unforgettable moments—one that would be recalled again and again.

For Christmas that year, our friends, the kids, came with a beautifully wrapped present. John, his usual gallant self, handed the gift to me. The kids all looked a little anxious and said that the gift was really for John. So I passed it back to him to unwrap. Big surprise. It was a bottle of Crown Royal in a lovely blue flannel sack.

John and I began to plot and plan how to be part of the joke rather than just the butt of the joke. We discussed how to sneak a little umbrella into the pastor's glass of water that he took to the pulpit each Sunday. We decided against that, but I do remember a little umbrella in a soft drink at a birthday party.

For one of John's birthdays, maybe the eighty-second or eighty-third, I gave him a surprise party. We had it at a friend's house. My children came in, as they always did for his birthday. The ruse was that we were going to stop by the friend's house for a quick visit before going to dinner. As we reached the door, it opened and the pastor handed John a drink while saying, "Whiskey, Mr. Pass?"

Such a small thing, this funny little incident, but a story that so many in the congregation became privy to—quite to the chagrin of John. But he laughed. He always laughed.

A merry heart does good, like medicine.

—Proverbs 17:22

The Valley of the Shadow

We had our own personal elder during the seven years of John's illness. This elder had been a friend since we came to the church in 1997.

It was an amazing thing to have an elder who kept in constant contact with us. He then reported back to the elder board, and they prayed for us. This was not something they did just for us. The elders took a list of all church members and assigned to each elder a group of members for whom that elder would pray weekly. Then, when there was a crisis, each elder would be in direct, regular contact to keep up to date with the elder's assigned members of the body.

The church body was amazing to us in those hard years. During the last three weeks of John's life, I never left the house. Our church brothers and sisters did everything for us. They brought food. I never made one meal. They brought groceries. They took the cleaning and picked it up again. They went to the post office and ran other errands. Just everything. I was allowed to focus completely on John and his care. Our elder was always calling and coordinating it all— making it effortless for me. And he came by daily there at the end just to check on us.

I remember sitting outside on the front porch with Vince, our elder, in June during the time when hospice care was beginning. In that initial time when John became so sick, my stress level was really high. I asked if we were walking through the valley of the shadow of death. Vince replied that he didn't know.

I now know that we were. The valley of the shadow of death is not necessarily a short journey. The valley was long and seemed never ending. And maybe the walking through it is what most of us dread. As believers we know that heaven is promised to be something so wonderful that our minds cannot conceive of it. It's the valley that we see our loved ones walk through that frightens us.

Jesus, the one who has been through the shadow and returned to us, was there for our journey. His presence was there in a tangible way. He sent Vince, the elders, the entire church body, along with other friends. We were loved and comforted every step of the journey.

> Yea, though I walk through the valley of the shadow
> of death,
> I will fear no evil; For You are with me.

> —Psalm 23:4

The Crown of Life

The end came suddenly, or at least I didn't see it sneaking up on me. The children and their families were both coming for Thanksgiving. I was in the throes of preparation. Everyone's favorite foods, side dishes, pies, the works. I even bought a playhouse for the back porch—one of those molded plastic ones, easy to move around. The weather was forecast to be in the high seventies, so perfect.

Both families, driving in from opposite directions, arrived within thirty minutes of each other. When they saw John, he was in rare form, laughing loudly, talking to the grandchildren and just being in his glory. He didn't have the strength to pick up the grandchildren, but we would set them on the seat of his walker and he would push them (slowly) around the house. They loved it, and each begged to be next. The night was so much fun!

John arose really late the next day, but I understood. The night before had been long, loud, and tiring. However, I noticed that he had hardly been up any time before he was napping in his chair. We had to wake him for lunch at 1:00 p.m. I was a little anxious when he nodded off during lunch.

After lunch, he went back to his chair, and everyone else went to the back porch so the babies could play in the playhouse. By now, I was extremely anxious. All this sleeping was *not* normal. I sat on the arm of John's chair and watched the babies playing; I was too anxious to leave John's side. Fear gripped me. My daughter and son asked, "Does Big Sir usually sleep this much?" I casually replied no, but there was nothing casual about the fear in my soul.

I have no memories at all of Friday. I was living for Monday, when the hospice nurse would come and give us a report—a report whose bottom line I certainly already knew.

On Monday, the hospice nurse told John, "You're going to be in heaven for Christmas, Mr. Pass."

It sounded as if he had won a trip to Disney World, and I guess the reality is that heaven is exponentially better than Disney World. John and I sat there together holding hands, talking about our life— how wonderful it had been and what a good team we had been. We sat there a long time like that, quietly digesting this information. Then, I got up to make the necessary phone calls.

Be faithful until death and I will give you the crown
of life.

—Revelation 2:10

Whistle While You Work

Throughout his life, John was always whistling. It was a happy tune, but it was a strange little tune. He would begin by whistling a familiar tune. I would hear him wherever he was—in the house, in the yard, in the car, in his office. Not too long into the tune, there would be an invasion by another familiar refrain. It is difficult to explain, but it was a repetitive lilting musical phrase authored by John, but easily recognized by those who knew him well enough to have heard him whistle.

John was funny, not always intentionally, but he was funny. And he was fun. John was almost totally uninhibited. Pictures exist of John that have no relationship to the reserved Mr. Pass of the early days. Pictures of John wearing a golf sweater over his robe, skinny white bird legs sticking out underneath. Pictures of John as the skipper of a houseboat—skinny legs and all. Pictures of him riding a Vespa, with a great big smile—legs covered. Always mugging for the camera.

Our daughter, Christi, resided in Dallas and chose to live in a neighborhood experiencing urban renewal—you know, old, but with potential! She lived in three successive houses with bathroom doors that wouldn't catch when they were closed. We would visit her. It was a normal occurrence for John to get up at night to go to the bathroom. Middle of the night. No one else awake. John would keep pushing the defective door. Thud, thud, thud, thud. And on and on. Christi would begin calling out, "Door dudn't close. Door dudn't close. Door dudn't close." I would be laughing hysterically at them in a duet with percussion and voice, almost a musical refrain!

John began wearing hearing aids about age seventy-seven. He hated them. They were an advertisement that his body was wearing out. John had always said that he was going to live to be one hundred. It looked like his mind would endure, but these were the first signs that maybe his body wouldn't.

After much frustration with his failing hearing, he went to the audiologist. John went so that he could prove to me his hearing was fine. When he came home, he reported that he had very little hearing loss—and that was only in his left ear. Additionally, the loss he was experiencing only kept him from distinguishing the first letter of the word. Really. He thought that was inconsequential? I pointed out that under his theory, if what I said was "sounds like a joke to me," what he might hear would be "pounds on folks to me." Huh? We had a good laugh, and he ordered the hearing aids.

My two children came to visit one weekend. After they arrived from separate cities, the four of us piled into the car to go to dinner. My children and I had an animated conversation going back and forth from front seat to back. John kept saying, "Huh? What?" I asked if he was wearing his hearing aids. His reply was "No, but you can't tell!" It was a crack-up! Of course we could all tell! He couldn't hear what we were saying. We never let him forget that funny response.

As John's disease progressed, he no longer had the breath to whistle. I missed his lilting, happy little tune. Like many other things, it had disappeared from our lives. Then one day, only weeks before he died, I heard it. John was in the kitchen having breakfast, and I was making the bed. I stood still and just listened, smiling. Poignant. I'll never forget that tune and how it enriched my life. Incredible. Literally, a tune now powered by breath from heaven!

> And The Lord God formed man of the dust of the ground, and breathed into his nostrils the breath of life.

> —Genesis 2:7

The Voice

John had a deep, resonating voice. A voice that still echoes in the hallways of my heart and mind. Along with that deep rich voice came a laugh that ricocheted and filled the air space in every room with joy. It was his voice that drew me to him. Well, it was his voice that drew lots of people to him. And children loved his voice.

I first met John when I was about twenty-three. He was on the board of a bank where I was a very junior secretary. John would come into the bank to transact business. The building was fairly large—both wide and long—with the entry doors near the middle of the structure. When John came in, we could hear him long before we saw him. We would hear him talking and laughing; we would look at one another and say, "John Pass is here."

John spoke to each person as he made his way into the area where I worked. He did his banking business with the president of the bank, who was also a personal friend of John's. I never thought John gave me any particular attention, or really even noticed me, for that matter. I was just another one of the people he greeted when he came into the bank.

I left that job when I was nearly twenty-six. About two years later, one evening my phone rang, and there was that unforgettable voice. I was totally surprised. John was twenty-two years older than me. He asked me out. I would not have been interested if it had been any other man.

But it was not any other man. It was John Pass. He wasn't just any man. He was a charming, charismatic man. A man with a great voice and a great laugh. I thought, why not, and said yes. It would be fun.

Our first evening out was interesting. We had dinner, and we talked and we talked and we talked. He was so easy to talk to, and he was such a good listener. The most interesting thing was how much we had in common. We had like interests—the common things in life. And so a second date was planned, and then a third, and so it went.

But I must say, it was his voice that made me say yes the first time. And his laugh became like an anchor for me. John and I would be separated in a room of people, but I would always hear his laugh and know where he was. It was a safety beacon for me. If I ran out of conversation or felt uncomfortable for some reason, I could hear that laugh and make my way to him.

Because of that strong clear voice, John was often called upon to read Scripture at Bible study. We attended the same small group study for around ten years. (This was the group, previously mentioned, which our pastor named The Old, the Rugged, and the Cross because we comprised the oldest members of our very young congregation.)

One night John was called upon to read a passage from First Corinthians. The passage addressed sexual immorality. John began to recite the passage, and in reading he made a small mistake. Instead of saying sexual immorality, John said sexual *immortality*. Well, I caught it right away, but no one said a word. John repeated it several times. Finally, I pointed out that he had misspoken, or perhaps he was just hopeful! Gales of laughter followed.

That voice was a magnet. It soothed me. It made me laugh. It warmed my heart.

> So, who has made man's mouth? Or who makes the mute, the deaf, the seeing, or the blind? Now, therefore, go, I will be with your mouth and teach you what you may say.
>
> —Exodus 4:11–12

The Vow

For better or worse, for richer or poorer, in sickness or in health. That was the vow we both took in 1984. Sometime about 2010, one day when John was feeling particularly blue, I said, "Really? Do we have to do them all?" I quipped to John that I thought it had been a multiple choice. The vow was *or*. Who knew it would be all! We both had a good laugh.

It was true though. I wonder: if we could look into the future and see it plainly, would anyone really make that commitment? Looking back, we see that we all had rose-colored glasses in the beginning. So it's not where you start, but where you finish.

And we finished well. We were great partners—great because we liked each other, great because we were friends. We were each other's biggest cheerleader. We had fun. And more, we were both flexible, as demonstrated by the fact that each time life took a turn, we both chose to accept the new circumstances and work toward a new normal. More than just acceptance, but finding joy in the dark times. It's easy to find joy when circumstances are good. The real test is to find joy when you reach the "or" in your life. When things are no longer better, but worse. Poorer is a bummer if you let it be, and sickness, well, sickness stinks. But taken as a package, life grows richer and has depth with each new mountain that you climb together.

But we only made it because we were a cord of three strands. To the best of our ability we lived a life of faith, which proved to us all that things do work together for good to those who love God.

> For this reason a man shall leave his father and mother and be joined to his wife, and the two shall become one flesh.
>
> —Ephesians 5:31

Joy for the Journey

Again and again, Scripture states "His mercy endures forever," especially in the Old Testament and particularly in the Psalms. I do not contemplate often what is meant by mercy. Oh, I know what I have heard in church, in sermons, and in Sunday school class. I know what we talk about in Bible study, but I rarely focus on it in my own life. Head knowledge, not heart knowledge. I accept that mercy exists or else the Lord would probably just vaporize me on the spot!

A few months prior to John's death, he looked at me one day and asked me, quite earnestly, not to pray for him to live. Such a request! I considered my words carefully before I said them. "John, I pray for God to be merciful to you, and we know that He is a merciful God."

John analyzed my words for a couple of seconds and said, "Okay, I can live with that."

It was true. I had stopped many months before praying for John to live. In Bible study one morning, the group members had asked me how they could pray for John. I thought about it before I responded, "Joy for the journey." And that became my daily prayer. My desire was for John to have a fullness in his life, a sense of completion. I did not want him to suffer, yet we know that God ordains our suffering—whatever that means! There are many concepts in Scripture that are difficult to understand, yet we have to accept them by faith. Verdell Davis, an author, says, "All suffering is philosophical until it's yours." (Davis 1994) How true.

So also are concepts like grace and mercy. If you have listened to many sermons, you have probably heard that *mercy* is God not giving us what we do deserve, and *grace* is God giving us what we do not deserve. These tenets of faith are easy enough to conceptualize. They are much more difficult when they are no longer philosophical, but a reality in one's own life. To truly understand mercy and grace, we need to be in a place where there is nothing else in life that matters. Nothing else concrete to hold onto. The mercy of God is not something He gives reluctantly—like permission we sometimes give our children: "Oh, okay, just this one time." Rather, God's mercy is extravagant because that is how He loves us.

When mercy is spoken of in Scripture, it is most often paired with the words "tender" or "loving kindness." Those descriptions tell us for certain that mercy is not something God gives sparingly to His children. He gives lavishly and generously—"good measure, pressed down, shaken together, and running over" (Luke 6:38).

My sincere belief is that when God heard our prayers for mercy for John, God's answer was a resounding "Yes, my child. And joy for the journey, too."

> Surely Goodness and mercy shall follow me all the days of my life and I shall live in the house of the Lord forever.
>
> —Psalm 23:6

The Wrath of John

John rarely got angry. I am not certain whether he had manifested a temper in earlier years or he had matured to a point where he controlled his anger. I do know that John had the perspective that little we encounter in life can be helped by ill temper.

However, there were a few times. One of the most memorable was during a Christmas Eve dinner when Christi and I tried to talk John into doing something he did not want to do. The story begins with Christi, Shayne, and I cooking an elegant diner. Typically, the three of us would convene in the kitchen chopping, sautéing, baking, licking the spoon, and other such culinary activities. John would sit nearby on a barstool watching; he would venture into the kitchen whenever we put dishes into the sink. He liked to say that he "batted cleanup."

I am proud to say that I raised two wonderful cooks. We loved to cook together. These hours in the kitchen were times of great joy and bonding for all four of us. The dining room table was set with china, crystal, and the prettiest linens. The entire family had tired of turkey and dressing, and after some recipe searching, we had adopted a new Christmas menu that consisted of a sumptuous standing rib roast and a yummy sausage dressing. The finished product was both beautiful and ever so tasty!

On this particular evening, Christi and I decided that John, "Big Sir," should carve the roast at the table. John voiced an emphatic "*No!*" as if the matter were not subject to negotiation. We begged and we nagged until John gave in. His resistance in itself was remarkable because usually it was so easy to talk John into anything we wanted. On this occasion, however, he was insistent, and he had actually become a little cross with us before he relented.

Christi and I prevailed. We set all the food on the table, with the roast in front of John. I lit the candles, and we sat down to eat. We were all dressed in business casual. John was wearing slacks and a new off-white sweater he had received for his birthday. John began the process of carving, still grumbling under his breath. As he carved, I noticed John had gotten something on the elbow of his sweater. Then, I realized the spot was spreading! John had his elbow in the candle! And while his sweater was not quite on fire, it was definitely scorching. At the news, his inflamed emotions began to match his scorching elbow!

John became really angry. He lectured Christi and me that he had told us he didn't want to carve and now look what had happened. Blah, blah, blah.

Shayne piped up, "Drop and roll, Big Sir. Drop and roll." We all burst into laughter, and I quickly took the roast into the kitchen to defuse any further fire or wrath!

Soon, John returned to his usual, more convivial self. Humor had doused the anger and left us with a wonderful memory and a line to be repeated many times in the future.

> A man who is slow to anger is better than the mighty and he who rules his spirit rather than he who takes a city.
>
> —Proverbs 16:32

Family

Yes, we all have family and the thing to remember is that we are part and parcel of all the craziness of our own family. There's always a nutty Aunt Ethel or drunk Uncle Jimmy in every family. I loved John's family, and I loved being with them. I used to say that they "were a mess." And, they were, but in a good way.

In our early married years, we celebrated Thanksgiving and Christmas with all of John's extended family – including an ex-wife once removed. Evelyn was the wife that John had been married to the longest and was the mother of his children. Life was simplified if we could all get together at the same time. God was right about divorce. It complicates everything, most certainly holidays!

Evelyn was not all that excited about having holidays with me in the beginning. I described her as aloof. She stayed on her side of the room, house, yard, party or wherever and I stayed on mine. I could see that she wanted it that way. John and I had only been married a year when Evelyn had a very debilitating stroke. It was life changing for her and for her children. While she did not lose her speech or her motor skills, Evelyn's mind was not as sharp as it had been. She was no longer aloof with me. Now she was solicitous!

One hundred and eighty degree swing! At family gatherings, baby showers, bridal showers, parties, and holidays, Evelyn would find me and put her arm through mine and want to walk around and visit with everyone. She liked to tell folks how much she liked me and how cute she thought I was. Talk about uncomfortable! The rest of the family thought it was hysterical. Evelyn would turn to me and say, "I'm not quite right any more, you know." It became one of my favorite lines. Mostly because I realized, even then, that we will all probably face being "not quite right any more" at some point in our lives! Priceless, endearing, and very honest!

When the entire family got together, we had so much fun. There was always loud laughter and stories of past fun. My own children and I loved being a part of something larger because my own family was much smaller. And, let's face it, my family just didn't know how to have fun like John's family. Food, really good food, was a part of all celebrations. J.T. was an awesome cook as was John's daughter, Sissy. My kids and I are also all good cooks, but we just stood back and let them take over.

J.T. was always "large and in charge." He was good at it and most family gatherings *were* driven by J.T.'s personality. He was inclusive of everyone who might be around at the time – friends, employees, or neighbors. Everyone was welcome!

Through the years we had many ranch parties. Ranch parties were the best – outdoors, plenty of fishing, rides in the mule-drawn wagon, barbeque, music, often a band and dancing. In the spring we had our annual "bluebonnet" party where we rode horses or pickup trucks down into canyons bejeweled with flowers. Lunch was almost superfluous as we sat under the giant live oak trees in the breeze redolent with the perfume only God could birth, sweet and intoxicating, the smell of bluebonnets.

John's daughter, Sissy, really had a way with words. She has a great smile and an even greater laugh, both of which she uses generously. Her way with words was colored by her West Texas drawl which painted her conversations with monosyllabic words drawn into multi-syllables. We love it when she calls her son, "Je –eff."

Sissy has been an extraordinary mother and now grandmother. She is an inspiration to all for the volunteer work that consumes her spare time. And, she is a matchless friend and was a great daughter. Sissy always puts the needs of others before her own. Sissy loves family.

John's youngest daughter, Cindy, is so like her father. She looks like her father and loved the same things he loved – fishing and Dallas Cowboy football. She loved being with her dad, but as life can happen, Cindy didn't get to spend near enough time with John, especially in the end.

At age seventy-seven, John had open heart surgery. Part of the diagnostic process was angioplasty. On that Friday morning in Dallas, all the children showed up. John was in great form and not really showing great anxiety. The doctor returned in fifteen minutes which told me, even without words, that the news was not good. The doctor confirmed that John needed open heart surgery and scheduled it for the following Tuesday.

The entire family returned on the following Tuesday – including a couple of adult grandchildren. Open heart surgery is long, over five hours. The entire family sat in the waiting room gathered around a tiny table and played black jack for what could have seemed an endless day. It was not. It was a day of laughter and the joy of being together, even in terrible circumstances.

Family. God created family. His goal seems to be that we can experience, in a very small way, the love He has for us through our family. The concept of God loving us more than we love our own children is a concept almost too ethereal for us to grasp. But, there it is. God created family – Adam and Eve, Abraham and Sarah, Joseph and Mary.

In the end of John's life, he was asked by one of the elders if there was any reason that he was not ready to leave this earth. When John answered that he was concerned about me, the elder replied, "God loves Diann more than you do." John was comforted greatly by that truth. I, too, find peace and comfort to know that I am a daughter of God. I belong to the family of God and He loves me more than anyone on this earth.

> But as many as received Him, to them He gave the right to become children of God, to those who believe in His name.

> —John 1:12

Do Something

We were living in a fairly large house on an acre in the center of Dallas when the economy changed—dramatically and quickly for John. A change in law had eliminated some of the benefits of real estate investment, taking many investors out of the market. That change, coupled with a bust in the oil business, brought real estate developers to their knees.

This downturn came in the mid-1980s during the Reagan administration. The reason for the oil bust (a drastic fall in oil prices) is unknown to me, but even now, in the oil country where I now live, people speak of that time as monumental. In the crisis, those in the real estate development business faced a glut in real estate. John owned a number of apartment complexes, maybe ten or more—about half in oil country. With the loss of jobs, many people moved out of the apartments and left for other parts of the country where they could get work. This was devastating for owners, because the expenses still continued even though the tenants had moved out. Maintenance, taxes, labor, loan payments. Instead of collecting a check, you had to write one! This event was known as a cash call. Not a small check either. And cash calls came weekly.

One of the catchphrases of the Reagan era was "trickle-down economics." It worked both ways. At the beginning of the downturn, laborers lost their jobs—and then ceiling fan salespeople, lumber yard workers, and it trickled down from there. At the beginning, John was not too worried about us. He did worry when he determined he had to put people out of work, but he felt personally that his "deep pockets" would keep us safe.

Many nights John could not sleep. He would go to bed at a regular time but soon awaken and spend time running numbers. He tried to find creative ways to turn this problem around. Eventually, sadly, John closed his business of over twenty-five years. Paying those negatives over several years had finally taken its toll. That meant 150 employees, some employed for decades, were out of work. John would sit up worrying and making plans. Who could he call to get those people employed? Trickle down had finally trickled up to the top.

Early on, when we were still living in that large home, it was Christmas Eve, and we were having one of our typical extravagant holidays. We were getting ready for lunch, and John received a call from one of his junior partners saying one of their subcontractors, who was living on a farm owned by John Pass Investments north of Dallas, was hunting to provide food for his family. He had just killed a beaver because it was all he could find.

John was just sick. We were about to sit down for lunch, but John took my son and went to the local grocery. John spent several hundred dollars on food for that family. He intended to deliver the food later in the day, after we had eaten lunch.

Ironically, while John and Shayne were gone, they left the gate open, and we had a knock at the door. It was a man in a pick-up truck asking for work. He said he would do anything just to have money for Christmas. I encouraged him to wait for John to return, but the man left. When John returned home, he drove around the neighborhood for an hour searching for that man so that he could help him.

We finally sat down for lunch. We had all lost our appetite. After maybe thirty quiet minutes, John stood up and asked if it was okay to take our prepared lunch to the subcontractor's family, along with the groceries John had purchased. We wrapped it up, and he was on his way.

John cared, and he did something about it.

Be doers of the Word, not hearers only.

—James 1:22

The Hardest Day

The hardest day was not the day John died, Wednesday, December 12. The hardest day was Saturday, December 1. The day began like any other had since the time we had learned that John's days were short. John arose about nine-thirty in the morning and came into the kitchen wearing his pajamas covered by a soft fleecy robe monogrammed with the words Big Sir. He also wore his bright purple TCU house shoes that had become a signature wardrobe item. They were the only shoes he wore that did not hurt his feet. Generally speaking, by the time people get to be eighty-six, they have pretty well worn out their feet, along with a lot of other body parts! We heard John's house shoes as they slid across the tile from the bedroom into the kitchen.

Each day John had looked weaker. His color was gray, but so was his beard and his hair, so I didn't take extra notice. His smile was bright and wide as he acknowledged my son and I. Shayne gave John a little pat, and I gave him a little peck. So began the day, another day in a string of odd days.

I remember little about most of the day except that later in the day Joe and Tina came over to watch the TCU football game with

John, Shayne, and me. Tina and I also put together a collage of photos of my grandchildren; I wanted to hang the photos prior to the grandchildren's return for a memorial service—which looked as if it would be soon.

Joe and Tina left at about seven in the evening, and the three of us sat there watching whatever football game was on the television. John started to gag intermittently. One of the hallmarks of emphysema is the excess amount of mucus the lungs make. There were always trash containers full of tissues John used when coughing up the mucus. As the evening wore on, John's mucus seemed to be increasing, and so was my stress level.

I picked up the iPad and began ordering Christmas toys for the grandbabies. Next, I ordered shoes for standing—standing in a receiving line at a memorial service. I stayed as busy as I could, all the while listening to the choking. I could tell that the mucus was thicker and more difficult to get out.

Finally, at about ten-thirty, I called the hospice organization and requested a nurse. John was not complaining, but I was beginning to stress each time he gagged—now about every thirty seconds. The nurse came, and now I can no longer remember what he said. I do remember telling my son, "I can't do this." His gentle reply was "I know, Mom."

The gagging continued through the night. Neither John nor I slept at all. At about three-thirty in the morning, I got up, took a shower, and got dressed. We were going to the hospital—I could not bear this another moment.

Shayne came in and asked what was going on. I told him that I had called the hospice provider and that I was taking John to the hospital. Again Shayne gently said, "Whatever you decide, Mom." I waited anxiously for someone from the hospice program to arrive. In the meantime, I called our friend to tell him of my plans.

The hospice nurse arrived at around five o'clock in the morning. He informed me that the only thing the hospital would do was put John on a ventilator! I was appalled. This was definitely the worst-case scenario. I did not think I could bear John's coughing and choking. It spoke loudly of his misery, and I didn't think I could bear to see that sweet man in misery. Yet the thing I was proposing was the very thing John did not want!

As Shayne and I sat there, still wrapped in the darkness, the friend I had called, Tom, came barging through the door. He said, "They are going to put him on a ventilator!"

I said, "I know, Tom. I'm not gonna do it." While I knew that, I did not know how we were going to get through the days left in John's life. The nurse assured us that they would get a hospital bed out the next morning and John would be more comfortable. The nurse also brought some drops, which, he also assured me, would help with the choking. I assured him that I was thinking of a new way to administer the morphine and antianxiety medication—one for John and one for me! We both needed it equally.

The nurse was right. The hospital bed helped. The new meds helped, even though I only gave them to John. If he was better, I was too! This was a new normal for us, a new low. I didn't know then that the hardest part was really behind me. The hardest day was over. From there the choking was much better and only returned a couple of times for brief stints.

Looking back, I now see that our perceptions of what will be the hardest thing we must do in a given situation is often a misconception. I had thought that the hardest thing we would face was the actual day of John's dying. God was gracious and walked with us through that long night of struggle more than a week before John died. God brought us to a place of peace. The peace that passes understanding settled upon our home, and when the day of final separation came, we were able to walk through the day with a serenity of love and peace.

Is anything too hard for The Lord?

—Genesis 18:14

The Big Game

The Rose Bowl. Could there be a bigger game? The game that can be described as "the granddaddy of them all". Yes, John's beloved TCU Horned Frogs were going to Los Angeles to play in the big game. There was much talk in our life about *The Big Game*. John was jubilant. He had waited for years to see his Frogs get to this place in history.

1-1-11, a special day for John. One of the players was a young man whose parents go to our church. That fact had made the year even more exciting for John. He got to talk about the game each week with people who were actually attending. John followed the season closely, watching on television and spending time during each game talking on the phone to anyone who would listen – and lots of people would.

A number of folks from our church were going, along with quite a few acquaintances of John and his son, J.T., who had also attended TCU. Because of his health, there was no chance John would be able to attend the game. The parents of the player were certainly attending, as well as many members of their extended family. They asked what they could bring John from the game. After some thought, he replied a program.

Game day was glorious. I made snacks while John watched all the pre-game. He fielded calls throughout the game from friends and acquaintances who were watching and wanting to share the excitement with him. All through the game John searched the screen for familiar faces.

They did bring him a program! It was signed by every single player! John was thrilled and surprised. He could not fathom that the young football player had spent his time getting every player to sign knowing that the locker room must have been a complete melee after the win!

In January of 2014, I sent the program to a man who was being inducted into TCU's football hall of fame. He loved John and I knew the program would mean more to him than anyone else. His wife had it framed in a shadow box and hung it in a place of honor – to honor TCU, John, and her husband- the Hall-of-Famer!

The big game. I think John has finally suited up for the most important game any one of us ever play. He's playing now with the rest of the saints, not the Horned Frogs. I am certain that some former Horned Frogs are playing too! I don't think anyone sits on the bench in heaven. I think there is probably always a cheering section. It is a game we each train for every day of our lives on earth. It is really the only game that matters.

> Do you not know that those who run in a race all run, but one receives the prize? Run in such a way that you may obtain it. And everyone who competes for the prize is temperate in all things. Now they do it to obtain a perishable crown, but we do it to obtain an imperishable crown.
>
> —1Corinthians 9:24–27

Saying Good-Bye

Time gives us perspective, if we allow it. Hopefully, with time we will have fewer regrets, not more. With time we should recall events with more clarity, not less. However, we all have a tendency to sugar coat the past or to make a person into more than he or she was in life. Sugar coating and elevating are not helpful. Neither are regrets. Survivors are required to live in the present in order to be healthy.

John and I did not say good-bye. We said everything else. We talked about the good parts of our life together, and we actually talked about our regrets, but not much. I know that we each probably had some regrets—words we had said, or actions not completed—but it seemed a waste to spend our precious time talking about things we could not change. In the end, our biggest regret was just the time we were losing, the future.

Good-bye was not necessary for John and me, but it was heartwarming to experience all the formal good-byes that happened in that last year. The first good-byes occurred when a couple of men came to visit John. One, in his seventies, had worked for John forty plus years earlier. That man had begun his own company decades later and was quite successful. He and John had remained friends throughout their lifetimes. The other man was a college friend of John's son. This man, when young, had gone to work for the older gentleman, and they had spent about thirty years together. Those two guys flew to West Texas to spend the day with John. They said they had decided it was a perfect opportunity to take some time, fly out, and visit with John, and so they made the effort. John was pretty fragile by then, and even though he did not need me to go to lunch with them, John insisted that I go. I had become something of a buffer because I knew when John was struggling or tiring and I could direct activities accordingly. The old friends spent several hours together with us reliving the past and laughing. Everyone in the room knew that this would be the last time. Those men would later take another flight, in December 2012, to attend John's memorial service.

Next came another man, with his wife. This man, forty-two years old, had been a boyhood friend of my son and at the age of nine had become acquainted with John. This man had called in early January and asked if he could come out for the day because he had something he needed to tell Big Sir. I replied of course, and they set a day. Like the others, they flew in and spent only a part of a day. What the man desired to tell John was how much John had inspired him, both personally and professionally. He had watched as John faced and went through all the challenges—in business, in finances, and in health. The man saw how those challenges affected John's life. He had seen John's optimism and his determination. The man had witnessed a life well lived.

Further, he wanted John to know that it was John's sweet acceptance of my children, Christi and Shayne, which led the man to marry his wife. He had watched as John fathered my children as if they were his own. John shared in the ups and downs of the teenage years and provided a college education. John was often

st person my children called to seek counsel during difficult
—and the first when they wanted to share the victories of life.

When this particular man had met a woman with a child, his
first reaction had been to reject her because he did not want to raise
someone else's child. Then, he remembered Big Sir and what a sweet
life Christi and Shayne had because of John's love and acceptance
of them. This man's wife flew in with him that day to deliver the
news that by following John's example, the man had not only found
success in his business but also established a fine relationship with a
wife and had three children. He gave John the credit. And he did it
in a way to greatly honor his benefactor. The man took time out of
his busy life to make the trip and deliver the gratitude in person. It
would have been much more convenient for him to have sent a short
note or even picked up the phone and called, but making the trip
in person was the only adequate way to share his heartfelt thanks.

Among the others in the long line of those bearing good-byes
was a couple who are close to my heart. I had known Deb since she
was about twenty-one, when we worked together. She had married
Bob a number of years later, maybe ten. Bob had been very young
when he met John. Bob had been fairly fresh out of college and
trying to make a new career start in real estate. Like most young men
who met John, Bob was fascinated with John. This young man had
picked John's brain, and John had generously made introductions to
influential people in the business. Bob was a hard worker, and he has
been successful in real estate, but I am certain he would credit the
encouragement he had received from John in the beginning. That
couple also flew into Midland for the day.

The last person to fly in specifically to say good-bye was another
man in his fifties who had known John for almost thirty years.
John had put him together with another real estate acquaintance,
resulting in a business arrangement. Those two, like the previous
two, were also still a team. John had worked with them selling

apartment complexes prior to moving to West Texas. This was not the man's first visit to us in West Texas. He had come a couple of other times. He loved John and showed his love by his presence.

Of course John's family came. His daughter from Dallas came for a weekend, along with her son and his family. Also, John's daughter-in-law and sweet granddaughter came for a few days near the end. His daughter who lived nearby visited with regularity, often bringing homemade goodies.

Like me, I don't think any of those people actually said the word good-bye. All knew—and I have to believe that John, too, knew—what they were coming to say. I know he felt honored. He said so. He seemed surprised. The fact is that our actions are more important than our words. The evidence was there in the lives impacted by John. Lives changed by watching a life lived to the fullest. A life worth looking back on, analyzing, summarizing. Time allows us to savor the sweetness of the one we were fortunate enough to have been blessed to know.

A man who has friends must himself be friendly,
But there is a friend who sticks closer than a brother.

—Proverbs 18:24

The Race

One year prior to John's death, the church conducted an interview with him. The elders made the request one day when they had come to pray for him. John's first response was absolutely not! He could not understand why they would even consider it. I was personally thrilled. And selfishly, I knew they would film the interview and I would have the treasure to retain for all posterity—and for me! John eventually came around and decided to do it. When asked for any advice he would give when looking back on his life, John's response was to encourage men to make friends. John valued the men in his life and their encouragement. He fully understood that the joy of friendship he had come to cherish was something he should have had all his life.

One of John's most beloved friends was Paul. Paul loved John. Paul once said that if he wasn't married to his wife, he would be married to John! That statement provided quite a laugh at the time. Paul had known John since John had lived in West Texas in his early career. Paul did not know John well at that earlier time, but it had been easy to rekindle their relationship in the latter years after we had moved to West Texas.

Paul and his wife were the ones with whom John and I had our last dinner out before John's death. Paul's wife had called, wanting to know if we would meet them for dinner at their private club. I did not expect John to say yes, but he responded enthusiastically that he would. As the day wore on, John began to worry that he would not have the energy to get ready or the endurance to make it through the evening. I encouraged John to let me call and cancel. I knew they would understand. No, he wanted to try to go.

The afternoon dragged on with John putting off the inevitable decision. He wanted to go so desperately that he continued the long process of getting himself dressed and ready. The process was not as daunting as it could have been, because a hospice caregiver had been there that day and John was showered and shaved. He only had to dress. Dress he did. That was the last time I saw John in street clothes (rather than his comfy warm-up). He was still looking good.

The night was emblematic of our relationship. Laughing, stories, fun. Paul encouraged John to have a steak. John had fish. Only I understood that John could not swallow steak. He was no longer able to swallow anything as solid as steak. His diet consisted of less-dense food now. But no matter—none of us were there for the food, even though it was excellent. We were there for the friendship. For the fun, for the laughter, for the love, one last time. I can hardly believe it now as I write this, but we closed the place down. That was a night when everyone had a story. We all participated equally. While we did not say it out loud, perhaps in our hearts we all knew that this very likely could be our last dinner together. What a way to finish!

I wish that each of John's relationships could have had that storybook ending. I can only be thankful that he had that one. In God's great grace, John was allowed one last dinner with his good buddy. Moreover, John seized the opportunity. He made a great effort, a supernatural effort that exceeded what his own energy alone could have achieved. The payoff for his effort is the cherished memory retained by each of us with whom John shared the evening. We saw him lean forward to cross the finish line.

> Therefore we also, since we are surrounded by so great a cloud of witnesses, let us lay aside every weight, and the sin that so easily ensnares us, and let us run with endurance the race that is set before us.

> —Hebrews 12:1

Bougainvillea

I couldn't believe that the summer had turned to fall and then the fall to winter. It was November, and I looked out to see that, indeed, there had been a frost, or two or three. I stood in my kitchen and saw the bougainvillea in the pot outside. It looked dead and very likely was. I had forgotten to bring it in before the freeze.

Such a beautiful plant, at least six feet tall and covered with luscious fuchsia blossoms all spring and summer. But not anymore. I had realized earlier that it was time to bring it in, but I had forgotten. Well, that is not entirely true. I didn't have the mental energy. I left it to die. You see, my beloved husband was dying, and I didn't really care what else died.

My sweet husband's passing was December 12. Sometime before I left to go be with my children for Christmas, I took pity on the plant and had someone come and bring it inside. Actually, it took two someones to bring it in, but I got it done and left.

January was cold, at least in my heart. I had returned to my home, in solitude. I remember staring at the lifeless-looking bougainvillea and thinking that it represented me. I felt dead. The leaves and blossoms were gone and optimism was pointless—dry branches with no discernible life.

Life was busy and overwhelming. I was trying to do all the things the law requires of those who survive the loss of a loved one—handling wills, bank accounts, cars, and countless other things. But I had John living in my head. I had all his wonderful counsel to fall back on. It was hard even so.

One morning in late February, I glanced over at the bougainvillea. Were there were bugs all over it? I moved closer to see what other bad thing had invaded my home. But no, they were not bugs. Instead, there were tiny green leaves all up and down the branches. I smiled. Just like me, the plant was coming back to life. All was not hopeless. All was not lost. Where there is life, there is hope. And for me, the sight of those tiny new leaves was a tangible sign that something I thought was dead—the bougainvillea—was actually alive. And that with nurture and time, it would thrive and blossom again.

Then He who sat on the throne said, "Behold, I make all things new."

—Revelation 21:5

Stoic

Dr. Smith had headed John's medical team. He once said, "When I get a call from Mrs. Pass, I return it right away because I know that she really needs something if she calls." Then he said, "Mrs. Pass is unflappable." And I was.

He was right. I now see that I was unflappable through most of those seven years. I had faced John's illness in the same way that he faced it himself, stoically. In those seven years, you could probably count on one hand the number of times I cried. I just didn't. There was never any doubt of how this illness would end. Emphysema has only one ending: death. No one ever gets better—just worse, day by day. So we accepted with God's grace our lot in life.

John and I lived each day and acted as if it were just like the one before, but we could both see that the days took a toll on him. And there were those bouts of pneumonia. I guess he had pneumonia at least once a year for those seven years. I was stoic, but I was afraid. The doctors told us that John would probably not die from emphysema, but rather from pneumonia or complications of pneumonia—such as, perhaps, a common cold that would turn into pneumonia and take him away suddenly. They were wrong. John did not die from pneumonia. It was not sudden. That it happened at all was too sudden for me, but I am certain that it was very prolonged for John. He went from his high weight of 190 (too high) to about 85 or 90 pounds when he died. He was frail and fragile. Breathing was so hard. The struggling for breath revved up his metabolism, and he could not eat enough to keep up. All my mental and physical energy was spent just trying to determine and prepare whatever tasty foods I could get into him to slow his weight decline.

On that December night when he finally left this world to go to glory, I was stoic. I did not cry. I looked across John's bed and said to my son, "Absent from the body, present with the Lord."

No real tears the next day at the funeral home—just exhaustion after weeks, make that years, of caregiving. Very few tears at the funeral ceremony. I think I would not have cried at all if my children had not cried. There's something about seeing someone you love crying that makes you cry.

Christmas. My son and daughter went home to have Christmas with their little children after making me promise to follow in a couple of days. I did promise because they had given so much and I was so numb that I didn't care where I had Christmas. There would be no celebration for me that year. And perhaps there never would be again.

Stoic. I spent the next two and a half weeks going from one home to the next, seeing both of my children, my mother, my friends. Stoic. Always stoic. Finally, on January 3, I piled my dog in my car and left for home. I almost made it, too. I made it to within thirty miles of my home when I began to cry. Huge sobs racked my being. I could hardly see to drive.

I cried day and night. I would get up in the morning and look at the single cup by the coffee maker and cry. I would cry throughout the day. I cried if I watched television or if I didn't. I cried every Sunday in church—huge rivers of tears that washed my face clean of makeup and sometimes left the entire front of whatever I was wearing soaked.

Stoic was gone. Seven years of stoic were over. I don't know if I will ever be stoic again. I hope I never have another reason to be. One thing I know is that those tears brought healing. They washed away the years of fear and hurt. They were tears of acceptance of the new circumstances. Tears of sorrow. Tears of a new fear.

When the tears were no longer daily, I was left solving the puzzle of who I am now and the questions of what to do with my life. The answers to those puzzles and questions have changed from time to time. (I suppose that is why those of us who have lost a spouse are told not to make any decisions for a year!) Though I still don't have clarity, I have more patience to await the answers. God reminds me, in blessings for each day that He has a plan and if I will wait, He will reveal it! I have come to fully appreciate that His plan is always better than mine!

I will give you a new heart and put a new spirit within you; I will take the heart of stone out of your flesh and give you a heart of flesh.

—Ezekiel 36:26

Getting Over It

Heal. Go on with your life. Get over it. Right. The people who say those things are the people who have never lost a mate or a child. Or maybe never had any significant loss at all. They make you feel as if you are wallowing in misery.

News flash. This is not wallowing. This is just misery. It has been two years since I lost my sweet husband. Sometimes it seems like it has been a lifetime since I have seen him. But the pain can still be so fresh. I never expect it. Music will almost always do it. Occasionally, it's a flash of a memory—something someone says. Or just seeing someone I haven't seen in a while. I can quickly be turned into a dripping sponge!

The whole process of grieving and healing is surprising. In the first few weeks after John's death, I was told that I had a "glow." Indeed, I would experience a sudden inexplicable exuberance. Then, I'd be plunged into the depths of sadness and despair. I spoke with a counselor, who suggested that I was no longer restricted as I had been for several years. Caregiving is a very restricted existence. I loved my new freedom until I would realize the reason I was free.

Joan Didion wrote a book entitled *The Year of Magical Thinking*. I had read it several years prior to John's death. A thought from the book returned to me. It was from a passage that chronicled how Ms. Didion did not want to give away her deceased husband's shoes, because he would need them when he came back! (Didion 2006)

I could relate. I did some illogical things early on. About a month into my new life, my son prevailed upon me to visit. After I drove four and a half hours, I arrived about six o'clock on a Friday evening. At nine the next morning, I left for home. Illogical? Absolutely! I couldn't bear to be at home, because of the loneliness, but worse than that, I was miserable if I wasn't at home. I knew John wasn't there, but he was more there than he was anywhere.

My entire identity changed in a moment. Within a few days, I was receiving mail addressed solely to me. I was so shocked. I had been Mrs. John Pass for thirty years. How could I lose my entire identity in a moment? I was no longer a wife, but a widow. I detested that title.

Thirty minutes. First, I begged God for just thirty minutes a week. I felt that if I could have thirty minutes a week with John, I could endure the loss. After a while, I began to ask for thirty minutes just one more time. I shared my desire with some friends, who asked if I would please call them if John came back. I laughed and said I would call not only them, but also the media! I now realize I used this desire as a coping mechanism. I knew that the Lord would not bring John back for thirty minutes, but the hope that He might got me through those first months.

Socially I felt totally lost, inept. I wasn't, but I was lost without John. John, who was always there. John, who thought I was cute. John, who laughed at my jokes. John, who anchored my life.

I had strange comments from both friends and acquaintances. When I was asked at work about three months after John's death how I was doing, another person inquired, "Have you been sick?"

I replied that I had lost my husband—which I *knew* she was aware of. "But that was months ago," she said. Yes, she was right. In fact I could have quoted her months, weeks, days.

Another friend commented that she was surprised that I was having so much difficulty in light of the fact that John had been ill for so long. There was no question that I knew for years that I would lose him to this illness. And amazing as the human mind is, no way can your mind jump ahead and deal with an event in the future—especially the death of one we love, one we spend each day and night with for decades!

Still another friend made the comment that I seemed to think I had a corner on grieving. This was in response to my continuing tears after only five months. She let me know that she had lost her father six years before and still missed him. Why do people think they need to quantify grief—or compare? It just is what it is and takes however long it takes for each individual.

Another thing. Decisions. I could make no decisions. I mean *no* decisions. I delayed or avoided decisions. When I went out to dinner with friends, I would just order what they did. It was so much easier than making a decision of my own. There were so many decisions to be made—decisions that were important, but so difficult to make at such a time.

Healing is a journey that I have not completed. I see that it has many rabbit trails. And many dead ends. Many U-turns. Oh, that it were a straight line.

> To everything there is a season,
> A time for every purpose under heaven: . . .
> A time to weep,
> And a time to laugh.
> A time to mourn,
> And a time to dance.
>
> —Ecclesiastes 3:1. . .4

Feeling the Loss

It is difficult to imagine those people who experience the loss of a loved one in a moment. My loss of John was slow, steady, daily. The blessing was that I could adjust to each new loss before the next one overtook me.

The first thing I can recall was that almost from the first diagnosis, John no longer had the breath to take out the trash. Now, that seems like such a small thing. But it was an irritating thing to me! For a long time, I was embarrassed at my reaction.

The realization came to me a full year after John's death that I was not angry because he could no longer take out the trash, but because he was ill at all! I was angry at the universe, and the God who made it, for taking my sweet husband from me.

Unfortunately, my insight only came after I watched a friend whose husband was terminal complain bitterly that "at least he could take out the trash."

I thought, "Wow, that's why I had been angry at John about the trash!" I was so very thankful to be able to suggest to her that likely she was not angry he wasn't taking out the trash. She was angry at the circumstances. But I doubt she agreed with me.

God is so good to reveal to us, in His time, the things we need to understand as we go through the difficult challenges of life. He does it so we can help others. In helping others, we help ourselves.

A major loss concerned our dreams for a special vacation home. We had been planning a vacation home in Fort Davis, Texas, about a three hour drive from our home. Fort Davis is located near the Big Bend area of Texas—at the end of the Rocky Mountains in another range called the Davis Mountains. These mountains are not nearly as high or magnificent as the Rockies, but they are very majestic, in a desert kind of way. Unfortunately, there were two drawbacks to building a home there after the diagnosis. One was that Fort Davis is at a higher elevation, where the oxygen concentration in the air is lower. The second was that very little medical care was available. We had already secured the land and were working on the house plans. Abandoning our goal was devastating to us both. This disappointment revealed to us the enormity of the effect the diagnosis would have on our lives. On the other hand, the loss of our planned vacation home gave us something to focus on rather than the illness itself. I can still see that little house in my mind's eye.

The losses soon came at a steady clip. The inability to fly was a huge one. We took our last flying vacation four years before John died. We rented the requisite oxygen equipment and were so pleased to be going to Oregon—a favorite place for us. Now, getting that kind of equipment for traveling just ain't that easy! First, you make the airline reservations, at the same time advising the airline that you will be using oxygen. This must be done six weeks in advance—not one day less. Then, the airline sends the traveler a form to be signed by doctors. John's doctors were three hundred miles away, so we mailed the forms. They signed and mailed them back to us. Next, we took the forms to the oxygen provider, who signed off. Finally, we sent the fully completed documents to the airline. Whew! Even I was out of breath when we finished the process.

The plane, oh the plane. Another adventure! The battery life on the oxygen equipment was four hours. Our trip from Midland to Dallas was one hour, and of course, we had pre- and post-flight waiting times. The next leg from Dallas to Portland was three and a half hours. Obviously, we had to recharge the equipment in Dallas to insure a full charge for the last leg of the trip. Have you ever needed to recharge anything in an airport? I mean *need* to recharge? Everyone is recharging their phones, laptops, tablets, you name it. No one was willing to let us get access to an outlet to recharge. They would say they were sorry, but they had to recharge. Unbelievable. We walked a very long way to find an available electrical outlet—which was really hard on John. Of course, we had to walk back too, but although we were stressed and exhausted, at least the equipment was charged. (I have found that in the years since our last trip, airports have installed many power strips to accommodate their customers.)

Once our plane took off on the final leg, with us aboard, we relaxed and sought to have fun on our adventure. John and I loved to play gin rummy on planes. And we played loudly and competitively for the entire flight. Well, almost until the end of the flight, because an unexpected event occurred. For a reason that I no longer recall, we wound up circling for twenty-eight minutes—which I do recall in full detail, sweaty palms and all. The oxygen equipment had a digital readout: a countdown to empty. Or a countdown to out of breath, if you will. Neither John nor I were making it obvious to the other that we were watching the readout, but I would catch his eyes darting away as I looked toward the equipment. When we finally landed, there were only four minutes left on that blessed machine. I knew it was our last flying trip.

Most of the losses might not seem as significant as that. And truthfully, most losses were something we looked back on. We rarely realized it at the moment we had actually faced a loss—the start of what would be a continuing deprivation. It was difficult to tell whether it could really be the last time we would do a certain thing, as we tried to be optimistic. We lost the opportunity of going out to dinner. Going to church regularly. John going to work. John driving. Vacations in places like Colorado and Fort Davis—too high in altitude. Oregon—too far away.

All the losses can be summed up in a single word—dream. The rocking chair dream. The dream that we would grow old and sit in our rocking chairs watching the grandchildren. The loss of the dream. Each loss was another chip in the dream.

Now, you're probably thinking that these losses were less painful because John was already old and such losses are expected. In your estimation he may have been old. Not in mine. He was vital and hearty. His body was failing, but not his spirit.

Nothing can prepare you for the biggest loss. The loss of presence of someone you love. All the other losses pale in comparison. Yet for those who believe, even that loss is only for a time.

For our citizenship is in heaven.

—Philippians 3:20

Conclusion:
Defined by God

God is so good. I thank Him frequently for the time He gave me with John. Certainly John was heralded by all who knew him as extremely special. God, however, places into each heart a uniqueness. We are "His workmanship, created in Jesus Christ for good works, which God prepared beforehand that we should walk in them." Each one of us is born with a job! God has laid out for each person things which only that person can accomplish. Not one other living, breathing person can do what you are called to do.

More than that, God walks with us through the challenges of life. For John those included broken marriages, failed businesses, bankruptcy, death of a child, and emphysema. He will not be remembered for those. John will be remembered for his smile, his laugh, his love, his service to others. All the other stuff, including the earthly success and failures, will be forgotten. These successes don't define us; neither do the failures. The reality is that we are defined by God and how He sees us. We are made in His image. As humans, we often characterize ourselves by our accomplishments, but again, God looks at the "thoughts and intents of the heart."

It is true that we are molded by events in our lives—or more specifically, our response to the events we walk through. There are things we need to laugh at, things we need to forgive. Circumstances may shake us to the core, but they must not shape us. Jesus Christ endured everything we are asked to endure—and more. In a song, David Crowder sings, "earth has no sorrow heaven can't heal." (Crowder 2014)

It's true. John Pass had much sorrow, many difficult hills and valleys. He will not be remembered for them. He will be remembered for his robust response. God healed him as John surrendered his life. And now, John has reached the pinnacle. John is in glory.

Take heart, dear believer. God has placed in your heart the ability to overcome the world. He will take your hand each morning and lead you through the darkness, into the light, and finally into glory.

> Now to Him who is able to keep you from stumbling,
> And to present you faultless
> Before the presence of His glory with exceeding joy,
> To God our Savior,
> Who alone is wise,
> Be glory and majesty,
> Dominion and power,
> Both now and forever.
> **Amen.**

> —Jude *v.* 24

Appendix
Lessons for Living

These concepts encapsulate what I believe are the key lessons demonstrated by John in the way he lived his life.

- Think of others before yourself (the first shall be last).
- Serve others.
- Laugh often and heartily.
- The little things often make huge impacts.
- Work hard.
- Never give up.
- Never compromise your integrity.
- Be humble.
- Treat all people equally.
- Actions speak louder than words.
- Don't grumble and complain.
- Be thankful in all circumstances.

The point of this entire book is to show the reader what these principles look like when lived out in a life. John loved people. People felt valued when he spent time with them. These are qualities to be desired in our own lives. These are goals to be attained, so that when one's life is complete, the legacy the person leaves will be, as described in regard to Abel in Hebrews 11:4, that *even though the person is dead, he still speaks.*

Bibliography

Carnegie, Dale. 1936. *How to Win Friends and Influence People.* New York: Simon and Schuster.

—. 2015. *Matching Quotes by Dale Carnegie.* August 15. http://www. brainyquote.com.

Crowder, David. 2014. *Come as You Are.* Comp. Matt Maher, Ben Glover David Crowder.

Davis, Verdell. 1994. *Riches Stored In Secret Places.* Dallas: Word.

Didion, Joan. 2006. *The Year of Magical Thinking.* New York: Random House.

Truman, Harry S. 2015. *Harry S. Truman Quotes.* August 15. http:// www.goodreads.com.

About the Author

Diann lives in West Texas with her Labradoodle, Daisy and has been a chaplain in the workplace for the past seven years. Through her work, Diann ministers to people in all phases of living and dying. She loves mentoring young women, travel, photography, and mission work in Uganda with her church.

CPSIA information can be obtained
at www.ICGtesting.com
Printed in the USA
FFOW05n1704161015